Learning English

Password to Skyline Plus

Workbook

von

Antje Malycha

Ernst Klett Verlag
Stuttgart Düsseldorf Leipzig

Password to Skyline Plus Workbook

von
Antje Malycha, Kierspe

Acknowledgements
The editors with to thank all authors, publishers and photo agencies which have given permission to use copyright material. Every effort has been made to trace owners of copyright material. Where this has not proved possible, despite repeated enquiries, the publishers would be glad to hear from copyright owners of material published in this book.

"The Lone Dog" by Irene McLeod, from *More Poetry, please!* London: Everyman 1995, © The Orion Publishing Group Ltd, London; "Fog" from *CHICAGO POEMS* by Carl Sandburg, copyright 1916 by Holt, Rinehart and Winston and renewed 1944 by Carl Sandburg, reprinted by permission of Harcourt Brace & Company

Picture credits
Bulls Press, Frankfurt am Main: p. 8; Fotoarchiv (Sebastian Bolesch), Essen: p. 10; Jürgen Kleine, Ammerbuch: p. 14; Mauritius (Durnrath), Stuttgart: p. 23; Erika Lüning, Lübeck, *Punch*, 16 May 1984: p. 24; *The Spectator Cartoon Book*, 1994: p. 26

Dieses Workbook begleitet *Password to Skyline Plus* (Klettbuch 51046), kann jedoch auch weitgehend zur bisherigen Ausgabe, *Password to Skyline* (Klettbuch 51043), benutzt werden.

Gedruckt auf Recyclingpapier,
hergestellt aus 100 % Altpapier.

1. Auflage A 1 [5] | 2004 2003

Alle Drucke dieser Auflage können im Unterricht nebeneinander benutzt werden.
Die letzte Zahl bezeichnet das Jahr dieses Druckes.

Internetadresse: http://www.klett-verlag.de

Redaktion: Louise Carleton, M. A., Gillian Bathmaker-Vollmer, B. A., Helen Smyth, B. A.

Umschlag: Christian Dekelver, Weinstadt
Satz: DTP-Verlag und Lihs GmbH, Medienhaus, Ludwigsburg
Druck: Gutmann + Co. GmbH, Talheim
Printed in Germany.

ISBN 3-12-510462-9

About this workbook

Dear Pupil,
In this workbook you will find plenty of material which will help you to use, practise and extend the skills you have learnt or are learning in your textbook, *Password to Skyline Plus*.
There are four parts to the book: *Grammar review*, *Working with words*, *Skills workshop* and *Media workshop*. The exercises in the *Grammar review* section are designed to give you practice in those areas of grammar which most often cause problems at this level. In the *Working with words* section you will learn more about how to learn vocabulary by trying out different strategies. You will also be able to extend your vocabulary and become more confident at communicating by using words in a realistic context. In the *Skills workshop* section there are step by step instructions for producing your own texts of all kinds. Model answers show you how to put these steps into practice. The *Media workshop* helps you to analyse media, such as commercials, films, music, videos, etc. and also to organize and carry out your own media-based activities and projects.
Whenever there is a direct connection between an exercise, skill or extract in this workbook and in *Password to Skyline Plus*, the page in the textbook is given in brackets (*SB* p. X) and the chapter is given in the contents list. However most exercises can be done or repeated at any time, for example, when you notice that you need more practice in a particular area.
All the activities are marked with a dice. The dice tells you if you should do the exercise on your own, with a partner, or in a group.
Whenever an example is given to help you, you will find this symbol: .
I hope you enjoy doing the activities and wish you success and a lot of fun with your *Workbook*!

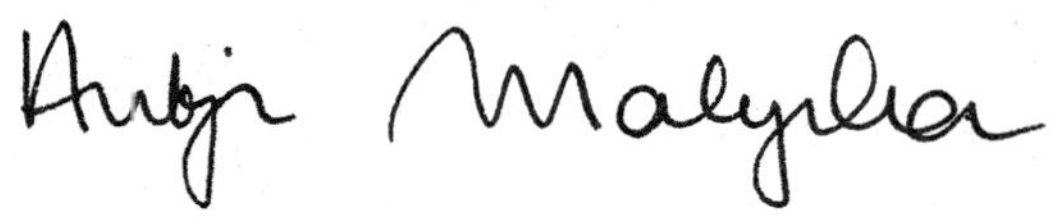

Contents

Media workshop

Abkürzungen in diesem Buch

SB	*Password to Skyline Plus* pupil's book
WB	*Password to Skyline Plus Workbook*
cf.	compare, see
e.g.	for example
etc.	etcetera, and so on
p. pp.	page, pages

Test your tenses

tenses

Read through the following excerpts from texts in *Password to Skyline Plus* and answer the questions to test your tenses!

a

"I have run I have crawled
I have scaled these city walls
Only to be with you
But I still haven't found
What I'm looking for"

"I still haven't found what I'm looking for", p. 88, ll. 5–9.

Which two tenses does the singer use in the last two lines, and why?

b

"When the year finished I went on a three-month special leadership course with the Army, but already I was having second thoughts."

"I'm happier as a volunteer", p. 96, ll. 24–27.

In the clause beginning with "but", does the writer refer to
- ❏ a series of past events?
- ❏ what was going on inside him when he was on the Army course?
- ❏ a completed process of thought?

c

"We've arranged to go to Norfolk to stay with Uncle Norman and Aunty Betty. Your dad fixed it up weeks ago."

"Keep on running", p. 12, ll. 23–25

Underline and name the different tenses. Briefly explain why they are used.

d

"Youngsters are terrified of school bullies, ... Manchester City Council has been consulting children aged 8–14. Young people from all social classes and ethnic groups were asked what most worried them. The findings have shocked officials."

"The children who live in fear of the yobs", p. 51, ll. 3–27.

Underline and name the different tenses. Briefly explain why they are used.

e

"They each picked up a text, gathered their books, and proceeded to the oak-paneled Welton Honor Room, where they had last waited to see Dean Nolan."

"Make your lives extraordinary", p. 72, ll. 6–8.

In the main clause, does the narrator
- ❏ stress a single completed action?
- ❏ stress activities in progress?
- ❏ describe successive actions in the past?

Why does the author use "had waited"?

f

"'One day, hard as it is to believe, each and every one of us is going to stop breathing, turn cold, and die!'"

"Make your lives extraordinary", p. 73, ll. 36–37.

In the main clause, does the speaker want to stress
- ❏ a prediction for the future?
- ❏ something that will definitely happen in the future?
- ❏ what someone plans to do in the near future?

g

"His dad was watching the news. He asked, 'Where've you been?' without turning from the TV."

"Playing God", p. 65, ll. 104–105.

The narrator uses three different tenses. Underline and name them. Decide in which case
- ❏ a single completed action in the past is described.
- ❏ a background activity in progress was not completed.
- ❏ an action has just been completed.

h

"I didn't fancy him, so I said 'no' nicely, as I still wanted to stay friends with him. But since then he has been really horrible, telling people that I'm a bitch, and it really upsets me. I've tried to talk to him, but he ignores me."

"Dear Mary", p. 76, ll. 4–10.

The writer uses three different tenses in this passage. Name them and briefly explain why they are used.

i

"'We have a lost generation of youngsters. ... Life is tough for them, and it is getting tougher.'"

"The children who live in fear of the yobs", p. 51, ll. 65–73.

In the last main clause, does the writer

❑ point out a process that is going on at the moment?
❑ describe the effect of a past action on the present?
❑ talk about a series of actions that happen one after the other?

j

"He braced himself as she stared at the duffel bag he'd taken from his folks' closet and stuffed with all the clothes and things he thought he'd need."

"Playing God", p. 63, ll. 5–7.

The narrator says "he'd" twice. What is it short for in each case? Briefly explain why it is used each time.

k

"If I were you I'd hop cheerfully about from foot to foot ..."

"Spock's Guide to Parent Care", p. 19, ll. 49–50.

In the *if-clause*, does the author refer to

❑ a theoretical condition that refers to the past?
❑ possible events in a person's childhood?
❑ a theoretical condition, i.e. one that is not realistic because the author cannot take your place?

l

"If you keep in mind that you're training your children's grandparents you won't go far wrong."

"Spock's Guide to Parent Care", p. 19, ll. 57–58.

In the *if-clause*, does the author refer to

❑ conditions that are unlikely to be fulfilled?
❑ the possibility that the reader may follow his advice?
❑ conditions that belong to the past?

m

"Then push in the door, she'll hear the bell, and this smile will snap on like a zipper unzipped. ... All of a sudden she'll be smiling like some beauty queen ..."

"The black-haired girl", p. 82, ll. 8–10.

In the last main clause, does the narrator refer to an event

❑ which he predicts as probable?
❑ which is a certainty?

What tense is used?

n

"Can it be
that it's happened,
that I'm ready
to step out of my cage?"

"Growing up?", p. 10, ll. 25–28.

In the second line, does the speaker

❑ describe a state that happened in the past and is still continuing?
❑ stress the effect or result of a past action on the present?
❑ express that something has been going on until now and may still continue?

What tense is it?

What has changed?

present perfect

The world has changed dramatically since you were born. Think about what has changed in some of the areas listed in the box below. Write six sentences (one for each area), making sure you use different verbs!

architecture • art • biology • communications technology • crime • family life • food • music • pollution • politics • population • school • sports • work

Hundreds of species have died out/become extinct.

Spoilsport

past simple/auxiliaries

Susie was to Mildred what a spoilsport is to a birthday.

1. a) Read the text "Mildred" (SB p. 21) again and make a list of the times when Susie behaved like a spoilsport.
   b) Write a short text in the past tense in which you explain why Susie was a real pain for Mildred. In addition, you could also include some auxiliaries in the past to make your text more interesting.

Susie used to + *infinitive*	She would + *infinitive*	She just wouldn't + *infinitive*
Susie had to + *infinitive*	She didn't have to + *infinitive*	Mildred wasn't able to + *infinitive*

2. Think of your own childhood and make a list of the times when someone regularly spoilt your plans or was a real pain. Write a similar text in the past tense in which you describe what happened. The expressions in the box will help you to structure your writing.

In the first place • Besides • Furthermore • In addition • Likewise

The unexpected visitor

past tense

Look at the cartoon and try to see the incident through the cat's eyes. Describe what happens using the past tense (past simple/progressive). Read out your answers in class.

"Celebrity" quiz

future perfect

You can have a lot of fun doing this exercise, as long as you do not take it too seriously! The idea is to ask a partner about some of his/her future plans and then make a prediction about his/her future on a small sheet of paper. You could use the examples below to give you ideas.
When everybody is ready, collect all the sheets, mix them up, and read them out. The class should then try to guess who is who.

By the year 2005 this person will have graduated from Harvard.
By the year 2010 this person will have become Professor of Mathematics.
This person still won't have had time to have a relationship by the year 2015.
By the year …

A mystery

tenses

1. a) Read the story in the box below, and think of at least five questions you want to ask to find out more information. Write down your questions around the story.

What was Julia doing in the room?

When Julia found herself in the empty room, she wondered why she had moved there at all. But then she thought of the time that lay ahead of her and concentrated on her plans. How much she had longed to be here. If only she didn't mind the room so much.

   b) Exchange books with a partner and answer your partner's questions.
2. Exchange books back again and write an extended version of the story in which you include your partner's answers to your original questions.
3. Read out different versions of the story in class and decide which version is the most believable.

Reflections on "Playing God" SB p. 63

tenses

After Josh has heard that his father also once had a dog their relationship changes.

a) Collect ideas about their relationship. The following questions may help you:
   - What **is** their relationship like **now**?
   - What **was** typical in the **past**? (e.g. used to + *infinitive*, would + *infinitive)*
   - What **has changed** since the day when they talked about his father's dog?
   - What do you think their relationship **will be** like in the **future**? (e.g. I wonder, I hope, I'm certain, I'm sure)

b) Rearrange the sentences and write a short text in which you talk about Josh's relationship with his dad.

In five years' time

tenses

Read the questions carefully, beginning with the one in the box and continuing in a clockwise direction. Try to answer them, thinking each time about which tense you are going to use. Then discuss your answers with a partner. If you can think of any other questions you would like to ask, write these down and discuss them, too.

Who do you think the young man is? → *Where is he?*

What was the young man doing before he fell asleep?

What is he dreaming of?

What will he do when he wakes up?

What might he be doing in five years' time?

How will his life be different from now?

What will he have achieved by then?

Superstitions

conditional

A lot of people in Britain think it's good luck when they see a black cat crossing the street. In Germany it's the other way round. In both Britain and Germany it is bad luck to walk under a ladder.

1. a) Try to write down three to five superstitions that are typical of the country you come from. Here are some ideas:

GB
If you find a four-leaved clover, it'll bring you good luck.
If you see a penny, pick it up and you'll have good luck all day.

D
If you break a mirror, you will …
If you get out of bed left foot first, …

b) How would you react if you were in these situations? Write one sentence for each of them.
- You are given a ring as a sign of friendship.
- You meet a chimney sweep on the way to school.
- You get to know an interesting person on Friday 13th.
- Your friends want to celebrate your birthday in advance.

Another country

conditional

How would your life have been different if you had been born in an English-speaking country, e.g. the UK, Australia, Canada, etc.? Write down five to seven sentences and try to link them with connectives. A few examples have been given in the box on the right.

If I had been born in England, English would have been my first language. Then …

First • Then • Later on • Next
At the same time • After that • Soon
Afterwards • So • Eventually • Finally
Last but not least

Afraid of what he might do *conditional*

1. Read the problem page letter opposite and try to guess the meaning of the words you don't know from the context.

2. Consider the different conditions that contribute to the boy's dilemma and finish the half sentences below.

   If the boy fails to get a place in college, …
   If his parents don't approve of him as a person, …
   If he weren't so convinced of failing, …
   If his three brothers were less successful, …
   If his "friend-girl" had appealed to his parents, …
   If his family had given him more comfort, …

3. What advice would you give to:
   - the boy,
   - his "friend-girl",
   - his parents?

   Write down one or two sentences for each person.

> I'm sure you're fed up with getting these kinds of letters at this stage, and I know you've handed out advice already on the problem, but I'm so worried. We've just finished our exams and my friend is absolutely convinced he's done really badly. The problem is that his parents have been fighting with him more or less all year because they didn't think he was studying enough. His three older brothers are all very successful, and the family's expectations are high. They have also warned him that he will have burned all his boats* if he fails to get a place in college, that there will be no second chance. So there is no point in appealing to them. My worry is the way my friend is talking. He feels his parents don't approve of him as a person, are deeply disappointed in him, and think of him as the black sheep of the family. I'm a "friend-girl", we've been close for years, but there is no romance involved. I just love him as a friend and am frightened by the way he's talking.

to burn one's boats to ruin one's chances

From *The Sunday Independent*, 25 June 1995.

Annoying situations *conditional*

1. a) Copy the grid below onto a piece of paper and imagine ten annoying or irritating situations at home/at school/with friends/etc.
   - List them as *if-clauses* in the first column.
   - Ask your partner to complement the main clauses in the second column.
   - Exchange books again and tick the adverb which applies most.

if-clauses	*main clause*	definitely	probably	possibly	never
If someone called me an idiot,	*I would ignore them.*	✓			

   b) Write out the sentences adding the adverbs you have ticked. You might like to read out your sentences in class.

   If someone called me an idiot, I would definitely ignore him.

Text quiz

conditional

When talking about texts you may want to speculate about alternative courses of action and character constellations or you may simply want to consider the consequences of a particular set-up.

Skim through the texts you have already read in class and make up six sentences for a text quiz.
a) Think about which type of conditional is required.
b) Write your sentences. Try not to make them too obvious.

If he hadn't clunked the spoon against his teeth, his parents wouldn't have complained. (Growing up, p. 10)
If she apologized to her father, he might let her run in the race. (Keep on running, p. 12)

Campaigning for improvements

passive

1. Work out a programme of what *will/could/should be done (conditional passive)* if you were elected as a pupils' representative at your school.
   a) In small groups, brainstorm ideas for activities, special events, clubs and meetings you would like to organize or improve.
   b) Think of arguments to support your ideas and then present your programme to the class.

   We think/feel/believe …
   We are sure/certain/positive that …
   We promise …
   We will do everything that …

   We are positive that the drama club will soon be opened again and that badminton matches will be organized once a month.
2. You could vote for the most convincing and promising programme in a democratic election.

Knowing more

passive

a) How well do you know Britain? Match the words in box A with those in box B and write complete sentences using present and past passive forms.

"Yesterday" was sung by the Beatles. (1 d)
Midnight's children *was written by Salman Rushdie. (8 b)*

Box A	
1) Yesterday	8) *Midnight's children*
2) Sherlock Holmes	9) *Coronation Street*
3) Shortbread	10) The Gunpowder Plot
4) William Shakespeare	11) Hadrian's Wall
5) The Armada	12) Lord Mountbatten
6) The Tower ravens	13) Oxford and Cambridge
7) The War Requiem	14) Pancake races

Box B	
a) the Beefeaters	h) Guy Fawkes
b) Salman Rushdie	i) the English Navy
c) the Provisional IRA in1979	j) Benjamin Britten
d) the Beatles	k) Sir Arthur Conan Doyle
e) Oxbridge	l) millions of viewers
f) flour and butter	m) Shrove Tuesday
g) Stratford upon Avon	n) a Roman emperor

b) Now read through the beginning of the quiz below on *Password to Skyline Plus* and add some questions of your own. Then exchange quizzes with a partner and complete the quizzes. Don't forget to use present and past passive forms.

How well do you know Password to Skyline Plus?	
1) In a Manchester survey young people	a her father
2) In Jackie's house the decisions	b) when Susie was 13
3) Mildred	c) what worried them most
4) …	d) …

Organizing a leaving party

passive perfect

a) List 6–8 jobs that would have to be done if you were organizing a party at the end of term. Write them down on two pieces of paper and give one of them to your partner.
b) Your partner ticks off some of the jobs (✓) on his/her note but doesn't tell you which ones.
c) Imagine that you are on the phone and have to check whether the different jobs have been done or not. Use *passive perfect forms* whenever possible.

– ask Julia's mother if we can have the party at their house
– invite …

– ask Julia's mother if we can have the party at their house
– invite … ✓

You: *Hi, (Alex) It's (Tina) here. I'd like to check whether the jobs for the party have been organized yet. Has anyone asked Julia's mum if we can have the party at their house?*
Your partner: *No, she hasn't been asked yet, but I'll phone her tonight.*

Nagging

imperatives/reported speech

What do your parents, teachers, friends or others say when they nag you?
a) Note down typical remarks in the *imperative*.
b) Write a short text in which you report these remarks.

Remember to …	Take …
Don't forget to …	Tidy …
Be home by …	Try to …

Sometimes I'm tired of being nagged. My mother is always telling me to remember to … and not forget to … . My dad wants me to … . Worst of all …

Mistaken affections

reported speech

Imagine you recently met an old friend, Ralph, and he told you about his new girlfriend Anne. Your partner knows Anne. Compare what you've both heard using the information below. Use reported speech and expressions of surprise.

You: *Ralph told me that he had been friends with Anne for ten months.*
Your partner: *That's strange because Anne said …*

Ralph's told you:

1. I've been friends with Anne for ten months now.
2. I first met her in the park after school.
3. I fell in love with her some weeks later when we were rehearsing for a school musical.
4. After the rehearsals we often stayed longer than the others.
5. Eventually I invited her to our house.
6. I was very excited because I didn't know how she really felt about me at that time.
7. When she realized that I was in love with her she admitted that she fancied me, too.
8. We've never argued since then.

That's surprising/amazing/incredible because …
That's strange/odd because …
Wait a minute, Ralph said …
You must be joking!

Anne has told your partner:

1. I've known Ralph for nine months.
2. We met at a friend's.
3. I immediately took a fancy to him.
4. He spent more time with his computer freaks than with me.
5. One day his parents invited me to his house because our dads work together.
6. Ralph was such a bore that I gradually lost interest in him.
7. I still liked him but I'd fallen in love with Alistair by then.
8. We're still friends.

That's surprising/amazing/incredible because …
That's strange/odd because …
Wait a minute, Anne said …
You must be joking!

An abrupt ending

reported speech

1. Look at the picture and prepare a short dialogue between three people which ends up with an argument. Try to include answers to the following questions:
Who are you? – Where are you? – What are you talking about? – How does the argument start? – Why is there a broken cup?

2. In groups of three, act out the dialogues. Avoid using swear words.
3. Sum up the main parts of your dialogue in reported speech and read your summary out in class.

A place of one's own

modal auxiliaries

Imagine that you leave home and move into a large house with some other young people. You decide to set up a short set of rules to make sure that life in your new house is different to your "old" life at home.

playing loud music – *doing the shopping* – *using the telephone* – *doing the washing-up* – *smoking* – *watching TV* – *playing computer games* – *doing the cooking* – *doing the washing and hanging it up* – *cleaning the windows* – *having friends to stay* – *taking out the rubbish*

1. Write your set of rules (no more than ten) using the ideas above (or any others you can think of) and a selection of modal auxiliaries from the box. You should write some of the rules in the passive voice.

Loud music may only be played after ten o'clock at night!
We must take it in turns to do the washing-up!
We never need to clean the windows!

can/cannot
may/may not
must/must not
will/will not
ought to/ought not to
should/should not
need/need not

2. Discuss your set of rules with a partner using the expressions below.
Don't forget, you'll have to explain the reason for each rule. Finally decide on five "golden" rules and present them to the class. The phrases below will help you.

In my opinion/view …	*I'm (not) sure/convinced that …*
To my mind …	*I would like to …*
I think/believe/feel that …	*I wouldn't like to …*
It seems to me that …	*It's a good idea to … because …*

Committing an offence

modal auxiliaries

Imagine a police officer/detective/teacher saw someone committing one of the following offences.

Driving without a licence

Helpful vocabulary:
driver's licence
personal particulars
registration number
owner
insurance
to go to the police station
to charge s.o. with s.th.

Taking a CD from a shop

Helpful vocabulary:
to search s.o.'s bag/pockets
the manager's office
personal particulars
to phone parents
to go to the police station
to open a file on s.o.
to charge s.o. with s.th.

Cheating in an exam

Helpful vocabulary:
to stop writing
examination regulations
to confiscate s.o.'s papers
to report s.th. to the headteacher
to be disqualified (from the exam)
to leave the room

In pairs, one of you should take on the role of the police officer, etc. and the other that of the offender. The offender should try to defend himself/herself but eventually admit his/her mistake. Both speakers should remain polite in this difficult situation.

May I …
Would you mind + -ing …
I'm afraid I …
You should(n't)/You ought to/ought not to…

Dilemma

modal auxiliaries

1. Read the following text about a moral dilemma carefully.

The school where Melvin's father works as a teacher has a lot of computer equipment. One day a computer and a number of electrical appliances were stolen from various rooms.

Melvin's sister is going out with the leader of a gang of youths who are thought to have specialized in selling stolen computers. The police don't know about their activities yet. Melvin thinks he has seen his sister copying keys and now thinks that she might have copied the school keys and handed them to her boyfriend, Dave.

Dave is seventeen years old and has already been sacked from two apprenticeships. However, he has now found a place as a trainee mechanic. He is said to be reliable and committed to his new job. Melvin's parents have never approved of this relationship.

Melvin's very close to his sister and doesn't want to let her down. Dave is all she has and she will do anything to stay with him.

2. What would you advise Melvin to do? Read through the five suggestions below and add two of your own. Now rank the suggestions from 1 (the best suggestion) to 7 (the least acceptable suggestion).

Rank	Suggestion
☐	Tell his parents.
☐	Report his suspicions to the police.
☐	Ask his sister to persuade her boyfriend to report the theft to the police.
☐	Ask his sister to break off the relationship.
☐	Talk to the boy himself.
☐	…………………………………………………………………………
☐	…………………………………………………………………………

3. Start with the least acceptable suggestion and explain your decisions. If possible, use *modal auxiliaries* and *if-clauses*.

[7] *Melvin shouldn't report his suspicions to the police because …*
[6] *Perhaps he could …*

4. You might then want to discuss your answers with a partner or in class.

Help and advice

modal auxiliaries/if-clauses

a) In pairs, read through the list of holiday jobs below:
waiter/waitress • gardener • farmhand • shop assistant • factory worker • child-minder • dog walker • swimming pool attendant

b) Your partner should choose one of the jobs and you should think of some advice to give him/her before he/she applies for the job. List the advice you would give in keywords. You should think about:
- *the best way of talking, behaviour and manners*
- *the best way of treating customers/the boss*
- *responsibilities*
- *previous experience*
- *skills, e.g. typing, driving, computer skills …*

c) Now form sentences using *modal auxiliaries* and *if-clauses*. The phrases in the box on the right will help you.

I think … should/ought to …
You'd better …
If I were you, I'd …
It might be an idea to …
Why don't you … ?
My advice is …
I would advise you to …

Partner: What advice would you give me if I applied for a job as a swimming pool attendant?
You: In the first place, you should be able to swim well and you must be physically fit.
Secondly, you must …

d) Now change roles: you choose a job and your partner should give you some advice.

Being together

gerunds

How would you finish these sentences? Write complete sentences, trying to use gerunds.

To me, old age stands for …
Isolation is …
To me, stars suggest …
Seeing you means …
School represents …
Being a teenager means …

Being a teenager means being ignored by most adults.

In profile

gerunds

1. Read through the verbs below and invent six to eight questions to ask your partner. Try to vary your questions and use different tenses. Then interview your partner and note down his/her answers. Make sure he/she uses gerunds.

to be afraid of • to practice • to remember • to be proud of • to be interested in • to be tired of • to avoid • to be worried about • to be good/bad at • to complain about • to look forward to • to regret • to dream of • to enjoy

What did you enjoy doing most last year?

2. Rearrange the answers and write a short profile about your partner. Use gerunds and try to connect your sentences.

My partner is … . She/He told me that she/he is looking forward to seeing her/his American pen pal in Atlanta this summer, although she/he's worried about staying there for six weeks.

Who does the work in your family?

gerunds/infinitives

1. Read through the *infinitive* and *gerund* patterns below.

Infinitive

make + *object* + ***infinitive*** without *to*

(not) have + *object* + ***infinitive*** without *to*

(not) let + *object* + ***infinitive*** without *to*

want + *object* + ***infinitive*** with *to*

ask + *object* + ***infinitive*** with *to*

Gerund

certain verbs + *gerund*
love/enjoy/hate/not stand/not mind …

certain phrases + *gerund*
what about/how about/it's no use/it's worth …

verb + preposition + *gerund*
look forward to/dream of/keep on …

noun + preposition + *gerund*
danger of/difficulty in …

adjective + preposition + *gerund*
tired of/interested in/fond of …

2. Think about who does the work in your family and make up six to eight sentences using the phrases in the box below.

to wash up • to vacuum • to iron • to mow the lawn • to do the shopping • to make your bed • to take out the rubbish • to tidy up • to lay the table • to walk the dog • to wash the car • to shovel snow
usually *regularly* *sometimes* *occasionally* *rarely* *never*

My mum sometimes asks me to wash up but I hate having to do it.
Usually my dad expects me to wash the car but I prefer driving it.

Famous people

relative clauses

a) Collect information about three famous people from the world of art, architecture, politics, sports, film, music, science, etc.
b) Write a two or three question quiz about each of them. Use the *relative pronouns* "who", "whose" and "which" in every sentence.

He's a person who died a long time ago but whose work is still famous all over the world. He wrote plays and poems, which show a great understanding of human nature.
(Answer: William Shakespeare)

c) Exchange quizzes with your partner (but don't give him/her the answers!) and do your partner's quiz.

Vocabulary test

relative clauses

Prepare a vocabulary test for your partner.

a) Collect ten nouns from texts you have already read in class and write them on a piece of paper. The nouns should match the subject matter of the text. They shouldn't be too difficult.
b) Write a definition for each of the ten nouns, using *relative clauses*.

It is a power which is believed to control everything that happens to human beings. It is not God.
(Answer: Fate, in "Playing God", p. 63.)

c) Exchange tests with your partner (but don't give him/her the answers!) and do your partner's test.

Understanding and learning new words

1. When you read a text you can often **understand** the meaning of some of the new words without having to use a dictionary (you might not always have a dictionary with you!). These techniques are listed on the strategy page on page 108 of your textbook and have been summarized below. Read through them carefully.

> **1** Word family – try to identify the root word, prefixes, suffixes or the different elements of a compound word.
> **2** Similar German/French/Latin words (but be careful of *false friends,* i.e. words which might sound similar but which have a different meaning! Always check whether the meaning fits the context!).
> **3** Context – look at the words /sentence before and after the new word.

> And don't forget – it is not necessary to understand every single word to be able to work out the gist of a sentence. Try to read over the new word and you will often find that the gist will become clear.

2. Now read the extract below from "Let's be tough on crime: teach children how to love themselves" (the complete text is on page 54 of your textbook) and try to apply the techniques described above. The three boxes on the left of the text have been filled in to get you started. You should fill in the boxes on the right with the German equivalent or a synonym in English.

Let's be tough on crime: teach children to love themselves (SB p. 54)

My job involves supporting *special-needs*[1] children in mainstream schools, and I'm sitting around a table with a group of seven-year-olds.

We have worked together for some months on their reading skills, and they are *progressing*[1] well. I decide the time has come to ask a crucial question: "Tell me, what are you good at?"

Responses[2] come in the form of startled looks, suspicion, confusion, and, finally, one voice expressing the unspoken thoughts of the others: "I'm no good at anything." *Low self-esteem*[3]? Absolutely. [...]

The Government's answer appears to lie in spending large amounts of public money on extending the prison service, on advertising *campaigns*[2] about the dangers of drugs and drink, and on creating rehabilitation centres. But these *measures*[3] do not work, as we can see from the statistics. ... Young people with low self-esteem are vulnerable. So what, if the use of drugs or alcohol is damaging to the body and may lead to anti-social behaviour? At least it *blots out*[3] the pain of failure. What value does life have anyway?

By Veronica Birkett, *The Independent*, 21 November 1994.

> 1 *special-needs* particular demands, i.e. pupils with learning difficulties

> 8 *response* –> réponse (Fr)

> 11 *low self-esteem* is the opinion you have of yourself if you do not think you are good at anything, and so you do not have a very high opinion of yourself

> 5 *to progress* ________
> ________

> 14 *campaign* ________
> ________

> 16 *measure* ________
> ________

> 20 *to blot out* ________
> ________

3. Here are some ways to help you **learn** new words. Read through them carefully and then see if you can think of any others. Don't forget there is not *one* particular method for learning and remembering new words. You should try and find the one(s) best suited to you.

- **writing definitions,** *If something is crucial, it is extremely important*
- **writing synonyms or near-synonyms,** *startled, surprised, amazed, astonished, astounded*
- **writing word scales,** *crucial > important > unimportant*
- **writing antonyms (opposites) or near-antonyms,** *low self-esteem vs high self-respect*
- **translating the word into German,** *vulnerable* verwundbar, verletzt
- **collecting collocations,** *i.e. writing down words which often appear together,* *to ask + a question*
- **collecting words in the same semantic field,** *school, teacher, classroom*
- ....
- ....

4. Read through the text below and try tc **understand** the new words using the techniques listed on the opposite page. Some help has been given on the left-hand side of the text. Once you have read the text, decide how you are going to try to **learn** the new words on the right-hand side of the text.

1 **county council** *(GB)* a group of people elected to govern a county

4 **cerebral palsy** disease caused by damage to the brain before or during birth. Sufferers have difficulty controlling their muscles and speaking

5 *to claim damages*
What might she want to get from the council to compensate for her suffering

5 *distress/*
6 *anguish*
What kind of feelings might s. o. have if they are bullied?

11 *to sue*
She is taking her county council to court and wants damages, so what might *to sue* mean?

How to see off the bullies

The case of a teenager who is taking her county council to court early next year may result in schools doing much more to combat bullying.

Becky Walker, 19, a teenager with cerebral palsy, is claiming damages from Derbyshire for the distress and anguish she says she suffered from being bullied at school.

Her colleagues in the school steel band – to which she was proud to belong – had got together and made her life so miserable, she says, that she left the band and lost confidence.

She is the first victim of bullying to sue and, if she wins, local authorities will have to compel schools to treat bullying more seriously than many now do. Bullying is a widespread and serious problem, as is clear from the results of the three-year Government-backed Sheffield Bullying Project, which will be published in January, around the time the case is heard.

Hemsworth Primary is one of the Sheffield schools involved in the project. Like others, it has its share of bullying. One of its pupils wrote: "Bullies are all the same. They hit you, kick you and call you names. If they don't like you, they say: 'You're dead after school'."

But Hemsworth differs from many other schools: it has decided to tackle bullying head on. Over the past year, it has not only acknowledged that bullying exists – a fact too many schools still deny – but has introduced a radical anti-bullying policy involving the whole school. As a result, bullying has been reduced.

By Jonathan Croall, *The Daily Telegraph,* 12 November 1993.

1 *to take s. o. to court*

3 *to combat*

12 *to compel*

19 *to have its share of*

24 *to tackle*

26 *to deny*

Youth – trouble or troubled?

1. The following words are taken from chapter four (SB pp. 51–54). Think of how you can sort them in a way that will make sense to you and help you to learn them. The techniques on the opposite page might give you some ideas.

Bullies, violent gangs, troublemakers and yobs threaten others.

bully • violent gang • frightening • terror • assault • crime • troubled • vandalism • hopeless case • troublemaker • wayward • probation • racial attack • yob • terrified of • fear • abduction • criminality • delinquency • bullying • threatening • secure unit • hostile • violence • prison • crime rate • drug/alcohol abuse • prison service • anti-social behaviour • football hooliganism • juvenile delinquent • conviction

2. You might like to compare and discuss your ideas in class or with a partner.

Word building

In English there are four important ways of forming new words:

1. **Add a prefix** to the root word *(see the table below)*
2. **Add a suffix** to the root word:
   - adjective –> noun + *-ness, -(i)ty, -ence, -th,* to show a quality/state, *good**ness**, certain**ty**, differ**ence**, tru**th***
   - verb –> noun + *-ment, -ion, -ation, -ision,* to show an activity/process, *pay**ment**, creat**ion**, organiz**ation**, dec**ision***
   - verb –> noun + *-er, -or,* to show a tool/s.o. who does s.th., *teach**er**, act**or***
   - verb –> noun + *-ing,* to show a process/result, *end**ing***
   - verb –> adjective + *-ing, -ed, -ive, -able, -ible,* *excit**ing**, excit**ed**, creat**ive**, believ**able**, divis**ible***
   - noun –> adjective + *-ous, -ic, -(ic)al, -y, -ful, -less,* *danger**ous**, artist**ic**, nation**al**, smell**y**, care**ful**, pain**less***
   - adjective –> verb + *-en, -ize, -ify,* *length**en**, popular**ize**, simpl**ify***
3. **Make a compound**, i.e. form words from two or more separate words:
   - compound adjectives : *good-looking, man-made*
   - compound nouns: *boyfriend, crime rate*
   - compound verbs: *to sidestep (a blow)*
4. **Conversion**, i.e. when a word in a particular word class is used in a different one without changing its form:
   play: verb (e.g. to spend time doing enjoyable things)
   noun (e.g. a piece of writing performed in a theatre)

1. Look at the grid below and fill in the gaps to complete the list of common prefixes. If you have difficulties, you'll find help on page 120 of your textbook.

root word	meaning of prefix	prefix	prefix + root word	root word	meaning of prefix	prefix	prefix + root word
certain	not / opp. of	un	uncertain				subheading
patient	not/opp. of			human	over/ more than		
honest	not/opp. of/ reverse						transplant
			misspell	act	between/ among		
write	again/back						co-author
eat	too much			Christmas	before		
			underfed				postwar

2. a) Choose one of the words from the box on the right and write it in the middle of a piece of paper. Now think of as many related words as possible, using some of the word-building techniques listed above, and arrange them around the word. An example has been given below to help you.

love • grow
cross • move
value

***inter**play*
***re**play*
play
*play**ground***
*play**wright***
*play**ing card***
*play**back***
*play**ful***
*play**er***
*play**able***
play (verb)
play (noun)

b) Check your words in a dictionary and add more words to your diagram. You might like to compare your results in class.

3. Think of other words that can be formed by *conversion* (see 4. above).

Outward appearances

1. Continue the word-field diagram by adding adjectives and nouns. You may use a dictionary if you want to.

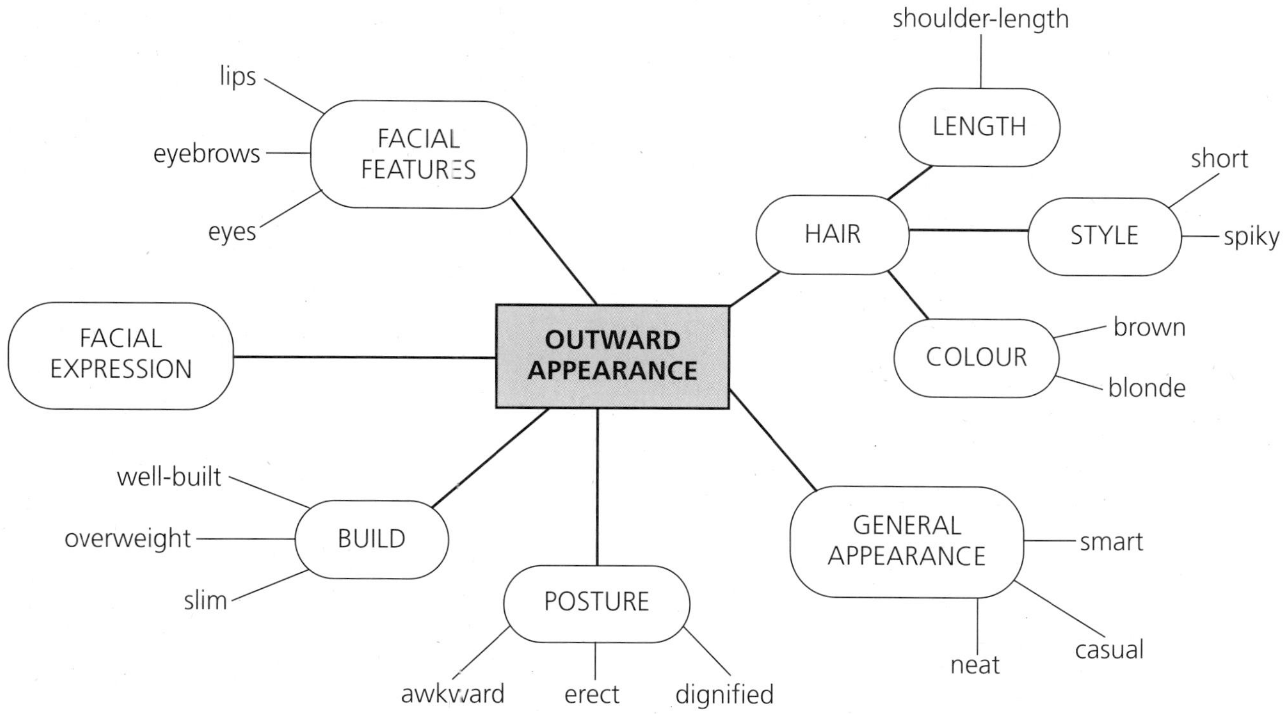

2. Describe in detail one of the people in the photographs on pages 8–9 of your textbook.
3. Describe the outward appearance of a person of your choice and read it out in class.

Characters

1. What are Mildred and Susan like? After having read the short story "Mildred" (SB pp. 21–26), decide which characteristics listed below fit Mildred and Susan best. You should give reasons for your answers. Look up any of the adjectives you don't know in your dictionary.

M malicious • manipulative • mature • mean • mild modest

I idealistic • ignorant • impatient • inconsistent independent • indifferent • inflexible • insensitive

L laid-back • lazy • lively • lonely • lovable loving • loyal

D daring • deceitful • decent • demanding dependable • desperate

R realistic • reasonable • rebellious • reflective reliable • reserved • responsible • rude • relaxed

E eager • easygoing • emancipated • embarrassing emotional • energetic • envious

D determined • different • disappointed • dominant dreamy • dull • dumb

S sarcastic • self-confident • self-conscious selfish • sensible • sensitive

U uncertain • understanding • unfriendly ungrateful • unhappy • unreasonable

S shy • silly • spoilt • strange • stubborn successful • supportive • sympathetic

A aggressive • amazing • ambitious • amusing annoying • anxious • arrogant • awful

N naïve • narrow-minded • nasty • nervous nice • noisy • nosey

2. Choose ten adjectives and describe what a person should not be like.
3. Make a similar list of adjectives to describe another character in your textbook.

Keep on running

Here are two important dimensions of personality: stability versus instability and introversion versus extraversion[1].

1. a) Take a close look at the diagram below and look up any of the words you do not know in your dictionary.

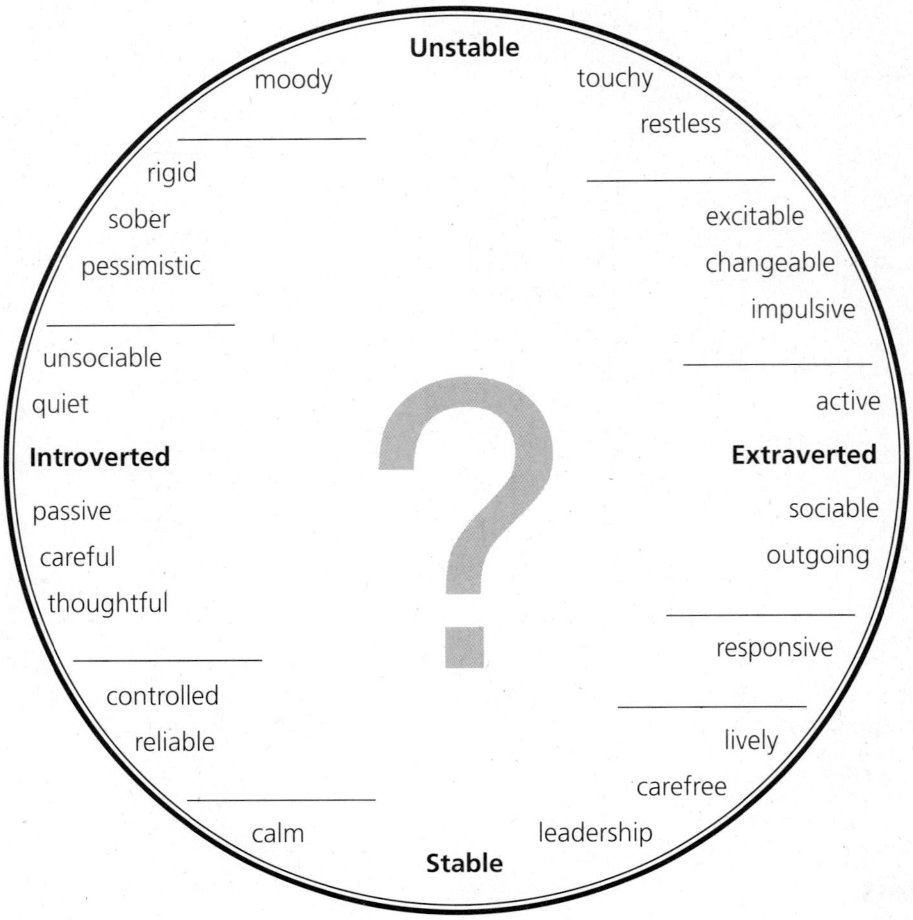

b) There are some gaps in the diagram. Decide where you would add each of the following adjectives:

aggressive • optimistic • peaceful • anxious • talkative • reserved • even-tempered • easy-going

c) Talk about your diagram in class and discuss your decisions.

2. Read the text "Keep on Running" (SB p. 12) again. Tick the characteristics you consider appropriate for Jackie in this situation.

3. Imagine a friend/your parents/your teacher had to write a short note about your character. What do you think they might say? Write a short text using the diagram above. Try to include some of the following adverbs:

generally • usually • frequently • sometimes • occasionally • there are times when • never
rather • quite • fairly • very • extremely

... is generally very lively but there are times when he is quite calm.

[1] Based on: H. J. Eysenck, "Trait theories of personality", in *The Companion Encyclopedia of Psychology* (Vol. 1) ed. by A. M. Colman, London: Routledge 1994, p. 626.

Atmosphere words

1. Sort the following adjectives according to how well you think they describe the atmosphere in the photo. Start with the most suitable and finish with the least suitable.

pleasant
depressing
relaxed
friendly
gloomy
cold
cosy
melancholic
romantic
warm
tense
peaceful
violent

2. Would you like to stay in this house during your holidays? Why, why not?

Guess what?

1. a) Read the following text and fill in the gaps using suitable adverbs and adjectives. Make sure nobody knows your words.

> One day I was walking ____________ along a ____________ street. It was rather ____________ outside and the wind was blowing ____________ through my ____________ hair. Right in front of me a ____________ woman opened a ____________ window and ____________ shouted some ____________ words at me.

b) Now paraphrase your words and ask your partner to guess them. You can paraphrase your words using:

- synonyms
- antonyms
- definitions
- scales

One day I was walking *quietly* along a *narrow* street.
I was walking without making any noise. (definition).
The street was the opposite of wide. (antonym).

2. a) Now read through this summary of "Mildred" (SB p. 21). Add adverbs and adjectives to make it more interesting. You can add words where you see an asterisk (*) if you want, or choose where to add them yourself.

> Mildred and Susie, two *American* *sisters, are like *strangers. The first thing that Mildred remembers about her *sister is her leaving home. Mildred is 15 years old when her sister *announces that she is pregnant and wants to come back. At first her parents are *shocked, but after many *discussions the *family, except Mildred, becomes *supportive and helps Susie prepare for the *baby.
> Before the baby is born, Mildred *helps and encourages Susie. The *baby is *named after her.

b) Compare your suggestions with those of your partner.

Emotions

1. Match the nouns in the box on the left with the generic terms on the right.

terror • cheerfulness
despair • kindness • grief
pessimism • reflection
depression • romance
pleasure • pensiveness
melancholy • fondness
worry • warmth • joy
sorrow • nervousness
gladness • horror • trust
contemplation • delight
satisfaction • seriousness
apprehension • closeness
contentment • gloom
longing • desire • anxiety
loneliness • friendliness

happiness	
thoughtfulness	
fear	
sadness	
love	

2. Copy out at least three nouns for every generic term and try to arrange them in scales.

gladness > joy > delight

3. Now form adjectives from the nouns for three of the generic terms. Compare your results in class.

Phrasal verbs

Look up the phrasal verbs in the two white boxes in your dictionary. Now fill in the gaps in the sentences with the phrasal verbs to understand the jokes.

to go out with s.o.
to come up with
to come across
to do without
to come down on s.o.

I .... a pair of twins last night.
Did you have a good time?
Yes and no.

"Did he remember my birthday or did you put him up to this?"

I'm afraid you will have to .... me at the party. I'm expecting a headache.

Father: Why are you crying?
Son: Our Maths teacher .... me today.
Father: Why?
Son: He .... the homework you did for me yesterday.
Father: What was wrong with it?
Son: He said I had .... the silliest homework he had ever heard.

Children never .... what will .... going to bed.

My children really .... the house. They never .... the lights.

There's only one way to .... children right – but nobody knows what it is.

to brighten up s.th.
to keep s.o. from
to put off s.th.
to turn off s.th.
to bring up s.o.

Collocations

Collocations are particular word combinations that frequently appear connected with each other.

crisis / crises

- ~ over
- ~ concerning
- to be in a ~

- political ~
- economic ~
- financial ~
- energy ~
- food ~
- identity ~
- mid-life ~

- to cause a ~
- to aggravate ~
- to pass through ~
- to settle ~
- to cope with ~
- to overcome

- acute ~
- grave ~
- serious ~
- mounting ~

Use a dictionary and note down as many collocations as possible for the following words:
• problem • difficulty • conflict

Truancy

Drawing a topic web – a diagram in which you structure a topic systematically – can often help you to organize your thoughts more logically (see SB p. 120).

1. Make up your own topic web to do with "truancy".

truancy

- Excuses for truancy
- Who is likely to play truant?
- Reasons for truancy
- What may pupils be doing when they play truant?

> • Write the main topic in the middle of a page and use this as a starting-point.
> • Draw lines to connect the different thoughts and ideas with your starting point.
> • Branch off lines to add related ideas, examples, illustrations, etc.

2. Now give a short talk on truancy.

> • Start with a provocative statement, a question, a short anecdote or a joke, or show a photo connected with the topic.
> • Arrange your thoughts in a logical order and use examples to add emphasis.
> • Don't forget to address your listeners personally.
> • At the end of your talk you can draw a personal conclusion or sum up what you have said.

Associations

1. Choose one of the topics from the box on the right and list all the ideas and images that come to mind.

search for identity

uncertainty

- search for identity
- jobs
- finding one's place in society

2. Write a short text about what this topic means to you.

Word groups

Sorting new words and phrases into groups is an effective way of learning new words.
Study these expressions (from "Graham's story" in chapter 7, SB p. 96) carefully and think about how to sort them into groups. You could, for example, make a grid and give the groups headings. You might like to discuss your ideas with a partner.

to follow an example	to get involved in s.th.	to put one's life in danger
to set an example	to go out of one's way to do s.th.	to cope with s.th.
to take a year out	to support s.o./s.th.	to be up against s.th.
to have second thoughts about s.th.	to be on the verge of doing s.th.	to hang out
to do a degree	to go nuts	
to handle s.th.		

Having an argument

Here are some expressions which you might find helpful when talking about arguments.

- to give s.o. a piece of one's mind
- to be right/wrong
- to hit the roof
- to fly into a fury
- to lose one's temper
- to come to terms with s.th.
- to answer back
- to contradict s.o.
- to be furious
- to tell s.o. off
- to calm s.o. down
- to be in a bad mood
- to go into a sulk/ to sulk
- to talk one's way out of s.th.
- to put s.o. under pressure
- to compromise
- to give in to s.th./s.o.
- to hurt s.o.'s feelings
- to put one's foot down

'I bet other people's parents don't put their kids under this much pressure.'

1. How would you explain these expressions?
2. Decide which words you would like to integrate in your active vocabulary. Copy out at least ten expressions.
3. Write an argument between parent and child, between siblings or between friends using the expressions you copied out in 2.

Paraphrasing

Sometimes when you are talking to a person in a foreign language, you do not know or cannot remember the right word or expression. At times like this you have to paraphrase. In this exercise you can practise different ways of paraphrasing with a partner. Student A should look at page 27. Student B should look at page 28.

Paraphrasing – Student A

1. Paraphrase the following German words in English for your partner so that he/she can give you the correct English word. The phrases on the right will help you.
   Gesundheit!
   (med.) Rezept
   Zwischenlandung
   gesetzlicher Feiertag
   Sonderangebot

English equivalents of student B's words:
ermäßigter Eintritt = reduced admission; *Geldautomat* = cashpoint; *Kunstaustellung* = art exhibition; *Beschwerde* = complaint; *Verabredung* = appointment (official meeting), date (with a friend)

It's a kind of/sort of …
It's s.th. which you …
It's what you use for …
It's the thing you can … (with)
It's what you … (with)
It's the place where you can …
It's when you …
You do/say it when …
It's s.th. you say when …

2. Describe three of the pictures below without the English word underneath them to your partner. He/she will then tell you what the correct English word for them is. (His/her pictures are in a different order to yours!)

fire extinguisher

ostrich

piggy bank

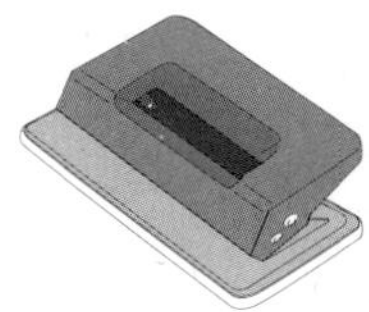
hole punch

stork

watering can

Expressing certainties

1. Proverbs are based on common sense. Read through the four proverbs about ambition below. How certain are you that they are true? Use expressions from the list to express your opinion.

to be positive about s.th./that
to have no doubt that
to be convinced of s.th./that
to be certain that
to be sure of/about s.th./that
to wonder why/what/about/if/whether
to question s.th.
to be uncertain about/of s.th.
to doubt s.th.
it is unlikely that
to disbelieve s.th./s.o.
to disprove s.th.

He that stays in the valley, shall never get over the hill.

There's always room at the top.

Better be first in a village than second at Rome.

Better sit still than rise and fall.

2. And now make up your own proverb about ambition.

Paraphrasing – Student B

1. Paraphrase the following German words in English for your partner so that he/she can give you the correct English word. The phrases on the right will help you.
   ermäßigter Eintritt
   Geldautomat
   Kunstaustellung
   Beschwerde
   Verabredung

English equivalents of student A's words:
Gesundheit = Bless you!; *(med.) Rezept* = prescription; *Zwischenlandung* = stopover; *gesetzlicher Feiertag* = bank holiday; *Sonderangebot* = special offer

It's a kind of/sort of …
It's s.th. which you …
It's what you use for …
It's the thing you can … (with)
It's what you … (with)
It's the place where you can …
It's when you …
You do/say it when …
It's s.th. you say when …

2. Describe three of the pictures below without the English word underneath them to your partner. He/she will then tell you what the correct English word for them is. (His/her pictures are in a different order to yours!)

paper clip

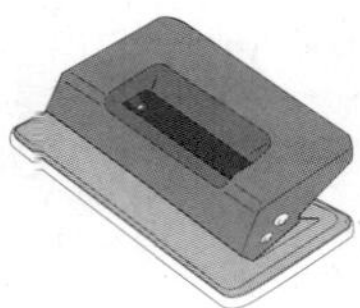

light switch

socket

peg

safety pin

hanger

From monologue to dialogue

Conversations are sometimes boring because they are dominated by one speaker. Here is an exercise which helps you turn a monologue into a dialogue.

1. a) Have a close look at the three different structure boxes below.

Interrupting
I'm sorry to interrupt but …
Excuse me for interrupting (again), but …
Sorry, can I stop you for a second … ?
Sorry, did I hear you say …?
Can I just add/say that … ?

Returning to the original subject
As I was saying …
Going back to …
To get back to what I was saying …
Anyway …

Changing the subject
By the way …
That reminds me (of) …
Speaking of …
Oh, before I forget there's something I wanted to ask you …
Funny you should mention that …

Turn-taking signals

The speaker
... asks a question
... makes a request/compliment/offer
... lowers the pitch of his/her voice
... slows down his/her speech
... lengthens the last syllable
... laughs
... pauses

b) One of you should now read out the beginning of the monologue below (not too quickly!) while the other one listens for and reacts to the turn-taking signals.

"I must say that I simply can't understand my parents. Why are parents so ignorant? If it wasn't for my mother, I'd leave and live on my own. You know, I wanted to work in France for six weeks during the summer doing voluntary work with the social services in Lyon. My parents had already agreed because they liked the idea of my doing voluntary work abroad. There were two of us going, but now my best friend has had an accident and can't go."

c) Now change over roles: the person who read the beginning of the monologue should now listen for turn-taking signals and the other one should read the rest of the monologue. After you have finished reading it out, you could try to continue it, but don't forget to include turn-taking signals.

"I know it isn't her fault but my parents won't let me go without her. It's not that they don't trust me but they're worried something might happen to me. I sometimes feel as if I'm being treated like a baby. And it's no use persuading them that I can manage on my own. Last year it was the same when I wanted to ..."

2. Together with your partner, turn the monologue into a dialogue and perform it in class. Use structures from the different structure boxes. You could also make a cassette recording of your dialogue.

Advice on chatting-up

Gilbert and Becky's first meeting leaves Gilbert feeling frustrated ("The black-haired girl", SB p. 82). What advice would you give him (or someone else) on how to chat someone up?

1. Try to give advice on chatting-up and fill in the grid. You might want to use some of the adjectives and phrases from the boxes on pages 14 and 76 of the pupils' book.

topics	*Don't talk about your family all the time.*
way of talking	
clothes	
what you say about yourself	
use of after-shave/perfumes	

2. Make a dialogue about "How to improve your chatting-up skills" and present it to your class. Use some of the phrases from the boxes below to request, suggest and advise.

Requests for action

Would/Do you mind ... (please)?
Do you think you could ... (please)?
Would there be any possibility of ...?
Could you possibly ...?
I'd be (very/most) grateful if you could ...
Can/Could I ask you to ... ? (I'm afraid ...)
I'm wondering whether ...
I can't decide whether ...

Suggestions/advice

What/How about ...?
Why don't you ...?
I suggest ...-ing
You could/might (try) ...
You can/could always ...
Perhaps/Surely you could ...
(If I were you) I would ...
Have you ever thought of ... ?
One way might be to ...

How to write an expository essay (see SB p. 116)

*You write an **expository essay** to make an idea clear or to convey a fact or a related series of facts. An expository essay is written in factual style and is usually in the present tense. An example of an expository essay is given on p. 32. Refer to it when you read the steps below and when you are writing an essay of your own.*

Expository essay

Function:	To make an idea clear To convey a fact or a related series of facts
Presentation of arguments:	The writer remains neutral.
Style:	Factual
Tense:	Usually present tense

Step 1

- Note down the topic.
- Add what you know about the topic, e.g. in a mind map, a diagram, a table, etc.

Step 2

Arrange your knowledge in a systematic order:
- start with general ideas and move on to more specific aspects, or
- start with specific aspects and move on to more general aspects, or
- arrange your information in chronological order, or
- point out similarities and differences between two related topics.

Step 3

Start with an introductory paragraph, in which you do one or more of the following:
- state your topic, or
- ask a question or a series of questions and promise to provide answers in your essay, or
- give a quotation to introduce your topic, or
- contradict a popular opinion ("Although most people believe …"), or
- briefly describe an experience you have had related to this topic ("When I was …").

Step 4

- Start a new paragraph for each new idea or group of ideas (usually three or four paragraphs).
- Use examples to illustrate the different aspects, if you want.
- Use connectives to structure your ideas (see p. 47).

Step 5

Finish your essay with a concluding paragraph in which you come back to the points made in the introduction. You could:
- end with a question,
- end with a quotation,
- outline possible consequences,
- suggest that the reader forms his own opinion,
- express a warning or a desire.

Write an expository essay on one of the following topics. Follow steps 1 to 5.

a) Friendship
b) Learning to drive

How to write an argumentative essay (see SB p. 116)

*The **argumentative or persuasive essay** is a very common essay form. You write an argumentative essay to express opposite views on a controversial topic. You can either take sides or remain neutral. An argumentative essay is usually factual and persuasive in style. An example of an argumentative essay is given on p. 32. Refer to it when you read the steps below and when you are writing an essay of your own.*

Argumentative or persuasive essay

Function: To express opposing views on a controversial topic
Presentation of arguments: The writer may take sides or remain neutral.
Style: Mixture of factual and persuasive
Tense: Usually present tense

Step 1

- Define the problem and give at least two different views on the topic.
- Collect information, arguments, statistics and quotations for at least two opposite opinions (make notes, a diagram, a mind map, a table, etc.)
- Formulate your own opinion on the topic.

Step 2

Arrange your arguments in a systematic order:
- state all the pros and then the cons, or
- state all the pros and cons alternately.

You may begin with the most or the least convincing arguments and then add further arguments according to priority.

Step 3

Start with an introductory paragraph, in which you do one or more of the following:
- outline the controversial topic
- ask a question/series of questions and promise to provide answers in your essay
- briefly present the reasons and the history behind the problem
- give a quotation or proverb.

If you intend to remain neutral, you could tell the readers that you are going to present both sides of the argument and that it is up to them to form their own opinion in the end.

Step 4

- Start a new paragraph for each new idea or group of ideas (usually three or four paragraphs).
- Use elements of persuasive style to present your arguments in a convincing way:
  - use connectives (see p. 47),
  - use adverbs to emphasize or tone down arguments (see p. 47),
  - use contrasting signals and subordinate clauses to structure your arguments (see p. 47).

Step 5

Finish your essay with a conclusion. You can:
- express your opinion,
- summarize your findings,
- outline possible consequences,
- suggest the reader forms his/her own opinion.

Write an argumentative essay on one of the following topics. Follow steps 1 to 5.
a) Both women and men should do a year's national service in the army.
b) All young people should do a year's community service when they leave school.
c) It is better to look for a job than to study.

Model essays: What is the reason for the increase in juvenile delinquency? Discuss.

Model essay 1 (expository)

Although broken families are often blamed for the dramatic increase in juvenile delinquency, the answer to why young people turn to crime is much more complex. In this essay I would like to look at the most important factors.

Firstly, there are certainly a large number of broken homes, where single mothers and fathers are not capable of giving love and guidance to their children. However the problem of child-neglect is certainly not restricted to single-parent families. It occurs in all families – partly because no parents are actually trained in parenthood but partly because parents no longer have time to give their children the care and attention they need.

In the second place, pupils are not given enough guidance at school. Teachers are often easy-going and let pupils get away with anti-social behaviour. They feel responsible for teaching pupils their school subjects but not for teaching them moral values or standards. Often teachers are not trained to deal with serious problems like violence and drug-dealing and on top of this parents frequently side with their children against teachers.

Equally important is the fact that many children live in squalid surroundings in increasingly anonymous neighbourhoods. There are not enough good playgrounds, sports clubs or youth clubs where young people can spend their free time under suitable adult supervision. Consequently many children spend a lot of their free time watching TV and videos, playing computer games or, increasingly, surfing the net. They often have easy and uncontrolled access to violence, crime and pornography. Society can hardly blame these children for lacking self-control in real life when they are shown this kind of behaviour via the media.

Economic factors are also partly responsible for the increase in juvenile delinquency. In families where the parents are out of work there are likely to be financial problems and discontent. If parents are busy looking for work or are worried about losing their jobs, they may not have the time or energy to give their children the attention they need. Similarly career prospects for young people these days are not good. If young people leave school and do not find work or get a place on a training scheme, they may feel worthless and bored. This could also cause them to turn to delinquency as a way of forgetting about their problems.

All in all broken families cannot be seen as the main reason for the increase in juvenile delinquency. Society as a whole is responsible and there are many equally important factors which need to be considered. However one thing can be said in conclusion: It is the overall lack of moral guidance and firm authority from adults and the resulting increase in child-neglect which is most responsible for the increase in juvenile delinquency.

Model essay 2 (argumentative)

Who is to blame for the increase in juvenile delinquency? Not us, say parents. Not us, say schools. Not us, say the media. Not us, say employers. Not us, say communities. In my opinion everyone is partly to blame. However, to my mind, the single most important factor is the lack of personal attention children receive in the family.

These days parents spend less and less time with their children. There are many reasons for this, of course: There are more and more single-parent families, in two-parent families both parents often go out to work, grandparents no longer live close by to help, more and more parents are unemployed and so they are worried about how to support their families. In addition, parents today are no longer prepared to spend all their time at home with the children, because they want to enjoy themselves in their free-time.

However, one of the most important ways children learn is by watching and imitating others. If parents are not at home or are too concerned with their own problems or too busy enjoying themselves to pay attention to their children, then their children have no way of learning what is right or wrong from them. Likewise children need personal attention in order to feel that they are loved and to give them self-confidence. If they are not given enough attention by their parents, they will look for it elsewhere. Unfortunately, it is often easier to get attention by behaving badly than by behaving well. Consequently children neglected at home often turn to delinquency to draw attention to themselves.

Clearly there are other factors which also influence children's behaviour and family life. For example, in many families children and parents do not talk or play games with each other anymore because they are too busy watching television. Children are allowed to play computer games and watch videos full of crime and violence. If a child spends all afternoon sitting in front of a TV screen having fun by "destroying" things, it is hardly surprising that that child may then go outside and destroy things in real life.

Admittedly parents alone cannot be blamed for juvenile delinquency. Communities do not provide enough facilities for young people at a reasonable price. Instead of being strict teachers in schools often allow pupils to behave anti-socially. And last but not least, prospects for the future for many young people are bad because there are not enough jobs or training schemes. These are all additional factors which can lead young people to turn to crime.

The way I see it, children and young people need moral guidance and support from adults, and especially from their parents, in order to learn how to behave correctly. They need attention and care so that they feel loved and gain self-confidence. As long as parents devote less and less time to their children, and the more children are therefore neglected in their families, the more we can expect to see a rise in juvenile delinquency.

How to write a news report or a news story

A news report deals with events of general interest and importance in an objective way. In a news story the reporter also includes his/her personal impressions and opinions and quotes from eye-witnesses and experts.

Step 1
Write a simple introduction in which you briefly summarise what your report or story is about. Giving answers to the five 'w's' will help you:
Who? What? When? Where? Why? (+ How?)

Step 2
Choose whether you want to write a news report or news story (see introduction above and SB p. 53).
Choose what type of newspaper you are writing for (see opposite).

Step 3
Write short paragraphs in which you add more information and details. After the introduction, start with the most important and interesting information and end with the least important.
Remember: people often don't read newspaper articles in full!

Step 4
Think of a good headline/title for your article.

Different styles in newspapers	
popular newspapers (tabloids) • short, simple sentences • basic vocabulary, frequent use of 'non-descript' words (e.g. *thing, place, do, be, have, fine, good, bad)* • extensive use of phrasal verbs (e.g. *to put off)* • frequent use of emotive language to stir up feelings and emotions	**serious newspapers** (quality papers) • complex sentences with subordinate clauses • more sophisticated and specific vocabulary (e.g. ~~put off~~ *– postpone)* • precise • emotions not expressed directly

1. Look at different daily newspapers. Select suitable articles which show
   a) the difference between a news story and a news report and
   b) the different styles between popular and serious newspapers.

2. Make a copy of the articles you selected in 1. and mark the following stages in different colours:
   a) headline
   b) introduction
   c) the five w's
   d) paragraphs giving more detailed information.

3. Read the notes below which are based on the story 'Playing God' (SB p. 63). Then, following the steps above, write
   a) a news report for a popular newspaper and
   b) a news story for a serious paper.
   You can add more information and details of your own, if you wish.
   Josh – quiet and introverted schoolboy – lives in small flat, Church Road – father unemployed – mother in training for new job
   unhappy at home – went out one day – wanted to run away from home – saw cardboard box next to bridge – heard noises coming from it – found five puppies in it
   took puppies home – found homes for four and kept one himself
   the Animal Protection Society heard of Josh's action – honoured Josh at their annual meeting last Sunday

How to write a 'plot' story

*In a typical **plot story** the emphasis is on action and suspense.*

Step 1
Choose an interesting scene/meeting/ experience with two or three characters. Make notes outlining the plot of your story.

Example: A short story called "The Runaway"

Step 1:
Rita runs away/parents criticize her about boyfriend/ gets off bus in dark road/hears footsteps/is frightened/tries to run away/panics, slips and falls/ turns round /sees that the person who was following her was …

Step 2
Start the action in the very first sentence.

Step 2:
The bus stopped at the end of a dark lane and Rita stood up to get off. "Sure you're alright love?" the bus driver asked as she stepped out into the rain. But Rita didn't answer. "Suit yourself," she heard the driver mutter and then the doors closed with a hiss and the bus was gone.

Step 3
Then describe the setting to create a particular atmosphere.

Step 3:
It was almost midnight and it was cold and wet. The road in front of her was dark and empty. Rita's eyes were swollen from crying and she felt tired and weak because she hadn't had anything to eat since breakfast time. But she didn't care. She just wanted to be left alone. By everybody.

Step 4
Develop the action step by step leading up to a climax. You could also:
- include a flashback giving background knowledge;
- include a turning-point in the middle which gives your story an unexpected direction.

Step 4:
Rita had no idea where she was going. She just walked on and on through the night. The rain had started falling more heavily now but she hardly noticed it. She walked on without seeing or hearing anything around her. Inside her head all she could hear was her parents' angry voices. And she could see their faces frowning at her.
Then suddenly, she became aware of footsteps behind her. Her heart started to beat fast and hard as she realised how far from the nearest houses she had come. There was no-one else around. She started to walk faster and faster. The footsteps behind her got faster too, keeping up with her, getting closer. "Don't panic," she told herself, without daring to look round. But in her hurry she didn't notice a hole in the pavement and she tripped and fell …

Step 5
Conclude with a surprise ending or leave the story with an open ending.

Step 6
Ask a partner or a group to read through your draft and make suggestions on how your story could be improved.

Read the example. Decide how you think the story might continue and write your own ending following steps 5 and 6.

How to write a 'slice-of-life' story

*In a **slice-of-life story** the emphasis is on character and psychology. This kind of story gives insight into a character's motives.*

Step 1
Choose a main character and an important moment in his/her life.

Step 2
Decide whether you are going to use a first-person or a third-person narrator (see SB p. 124)

- The first-person narrator is a character in the text who tells the reader what he/she experiences, thinks and feels, ("I"). This kind of narrator has a limited point of view.
- The third-person narrator is not a character in the story, but stands outside it. This kind of narrator refers to the characters as *he/she/they*. There are two types of third-person narrator:
  - the *omniscient* narrator, who knows everything about the characters and has unlimited insight into their characters;
  - the *selective third-person* narrator, who presents the story through the eyes of one character and has limited insight into the characters.

Step 3
Describe the setting in detail to create a particular atmosphere. Use adjectives and adverbs to make it clear to the reader what the protagonist (main character) is feeling, seeing, hearing, etc.

Step 4
Describe the different reactions, opinions and motives of the other characters.

Step 5
Concentrate on thoughts and feelings, not on plot and suspense.

Step 6
Finish with an open ending.

Use the information below to write a slice-of-life story about Sarah Cook, 13, who became known as the 'child-bride'. Think about using flashbacks or other stylistic devices to make your story more interesting.

The child-bride

- Adrian Cook and his wife Jackie take their children on holiday to Turkey in September 1995.
- The Cooks get to like Turkish pastries, Turkish lifestyle, people and weather.
- Sarah (12) meets Musa Komeagac, the young waiter who serves the family on holiday.
- Sarah has never had a boyfriend before
- Sarah cries a lot when she is back in England. She runs up a £1,000 phone bill.
- Sarah thinks about Musa.
- In October 1995 Sarah returns to Turkey to be married.
- Under Islamic law the age of consent for sex and marriage is puberty, which is in harmony with the biological transition from childhood to adulthood.
- Sarah is married to Musa, an 18-year-old unemployed waiter in Kahramanmaras, southern Turkey, under Islamic law.
- Ali Sezal, mayor of Kahramanmaras: "Girls mature quickly in the desert."
- Sarah's parents approve of their daughter's marriage.
- Jackie Cook denies rumours that she has sold her daughter for 15 camels as 'complete rubbish'.
- When Sarah doesn't return from the half-term holiday in October 1995, her headmaster raises the case with the Welfare Office at Social Services.
- The Social Services visit the Cooks but decide not to take action as long as Musa's parents write letters promising to look after Sarah.
- Following pressure from politicians Musa is arrested and sent to prison on charge of statutory rape which can lead to 6 years' imprisonment.
- Imprisoned Musa becomes a star on prime time Turkish TV, claiming that Sarah was already pregnant.
- Sarah is officially ordered home and made a ward of court.
- Selim Sumen, Musa's lawyer: "If Sarah leaves, Musa will probably be found guilty. If she stays, a legally recognised marriage might be arranged when she is 14."
- Sarah claims she feels ugly in Britain and never wants to come back.
- Sarah threatens to go on hunger strike if forced to return to Britain.
- Turkish newspapers celebrate Musa's and Sarah's love as a new Romeo and Juliet romance.
- Jackie Cook persuades her daughter to return to Britain where she is taken into care.
- Neighbours: "What Sarah wants, she gets."
- Natalie Webb, 13, Sarah's friend: "Sarah was always strong-willed and knew what she wanted. But everyone was horrible to her because she was fat and had ginger hair."

How to write a summary of a fictional text

A summary is a carefully planned and concise way of informing others about the most important points in a text. It is factual in style and is written in the present tense. In a summary, you do not express your personal opinion and you do not give details or examples or quote directly from the text. The following steps will help you summarize fictional texts correctly.

Step 1
Briefly describe the setting and the characters.

Example: A summary of 'Romeo and Juliet' by William Shakespeare

Step 1

setting:
place: Verona
time: 16th century, 5 days in mid-July

characters:
Romeo Montague
Juliet Capulet
Friar Lawrence
Prince of Verona
Kinsmen (relatives)
Friends & servants

Step 2
Briefly describe the plot (what happens and how the events are connected).

Step 2: The plot

- There is a family feud between the Capulets and the Montagues.
- Romeo and Juliet meet at a ball and fall passionately in love.
- They are secretly married by Friar Lawrence, who wants to bring the two families back together.
- Romeo's best friend is killed in a fight and Romeo kills the killer (one of Juliet's kinsmen) to avenge his best friend's death.
- Romeo is banished from Verona and hides in Mantua.
- Juliet's father insists she must marry Paris immediately.
- Friar Lawrence gives Juliet a drug that will make her appear dead for two days and arranges for Romeo to come and fetch her from the family vault.
- Juliet takes the drug the evening before her wedding to Paris.
- Romeo hears that Juliet is dead, but he doesn't receive the news from Friar Lawrence.
- Romeo goes to Juliet's tomb and kills himself because he thinks she is really dead.
- When Juliet wakes up, she sees that Romeo is dead and kills herself.

Step 3
- Choose suitable words and phrases to use in your summary, e.g.:
  - *the scene/passage/story/action*
  - *to take place in, to be set in, to deal with, to display*
  - *in the present/past/future*
  - *the atmosphere/the characters*
  - *to create, to evoke (an atmosphere/emotion)*
  - *plot development/exposition/rising action / climax/turning-point/denouement*
- Link your sentences with connectives (see page 47).

The play is set in Verona in the 16th century. It takes place over five days in mid-July. The main characters in the play are Romeo, a Montague, and Juliet, a Capulet. Their families, the Capulets and the Montagues, are having a feud.
Romeo and Juliet meet at a ball and fall passionately in love. They are secretly married by Friar Lawrence who hopes to end the feud by bringing the two families together.
However, there is a fight in which Romeo's best friend is killed by one of Juliet's kinsmen only to be killed by Romeo in revenge. As a result, Romeo is banished from Verona and goes to hide in Mantua. At the same time Juliet's father, ignorant of Juliet's marriage to Romeo, decides Juliet must marry Paris immediately. In her despair Juliet seeks help from Friar Lawrence. He gives her a drug to take that will make her appear dead for two days. He arranges for Romeo to be informed and to come and take Juliet away with him when she wakes up.
Juliet takes the drug on the evening before her wedding to Paris. But Romeo only hears of his wife's death and not that she has taken a sleeping potion. When he sees her apparently dead in the tomb he kills himself.
In the end, when Juliet finally wakes up and discovers Romeo dead at her side, she kills herself with his dagger.

Now write a summary of a novel or short story you have read recently and present it to your class.

How to write a summary of a non-fictional text

A summary is a carefully planned and concise way of informing others about the most important points in a text. It is factual in style and is written in the present tense. In a summary you do not express your personal opinion and you do not give details or examples or quote directly from the text. The following steps will help you summarize non-fictional texts correctly.

Step 1
Note the main ideas, facts or arguments in the text:
- in a list of key words
- by writing sentences summarizing each of the most important points

Example: "Let's be tough on crime" by Veronica Birkett, SB p. 54

Step 1
- special-needs children (and other young people) have low self-esteem
- low self-esteem is the reason for the explosion in the crime rate and in drug and alcohol abuse
- government policies have failed
- ways must be found to ensure that children receive positive empowering messages from adults in early childhood
- ways of helping children to feel good about themselves

Step 2
Introduce each point with a verb which describes the writer's intention. You can choose from the verbs below.
- *to introduce, to open with*
- *to outline, to present, to show*
- *to mention, to point out, to explain, to illustrate*
- *to emphasize, to underline*
- *to agree with, to confirm, to prove a point by*
- *to complain about/that, to doubt, to disagree, to criticize, to disapprove of s.th., to warn s.o. about s.th.*
- *to suggest, to put forward an argument, to claim, to demand*
- *to conclude (with), to close (with), to finish (with)*

Step 3
Link your sentences using connectives (see page 47).

Steps 2 & 3

The article describes how crime and drug abuse could be reduced if young people were taught to respect themselves. To begin with the author describes how she has experienced a lack of self-esteem in special-needs children. She goes on to blame this lack of self-esteem for the increase in the crime rate and in drug abuse amongst young people. She points out that government attempts to solve the problem have failed. She demands that ways be found of giving children positive feelings about themselves from an early age. Accordingly she suggests a number of ways in which this could be done. She concludes by saying that the world would then be a safer place to live in.

Read the text 'Tell the birds about family life', SB p. 71 and write a summary of it.

How to write poems

1. Lone Dog

This is the first stanza of Irene McLeod's poem Lone Dog.

Lone Dog
I'm a lean dog, a keen dog, a wild dog, and lone;
I'm a rough dog, a tough dog, hunting on my own;
I'm a bad dog, a mad dog, teasing silly sheep;
I love to sit and bay the moon, to keep fat souls from sleep.

By Irene McLeod, *More Poetry please!*, London: Everyman, 1995.

The use of assonance (lean/keen, rough/tough, bad/mad), the simple rhyme pattern (aabb) and the shift to iambic feet in the last line make the poem very expressive.

a) Choose a wild animal or a pet and write down as many suitable adjectives as possible to go with it. If they rhyme, so much the better (e.g. *proud / loud*).

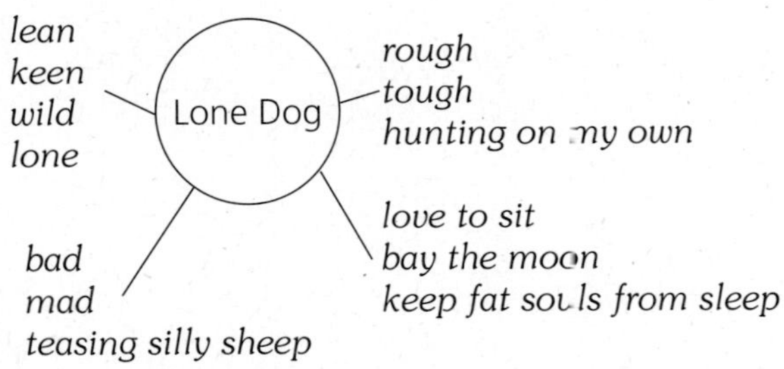

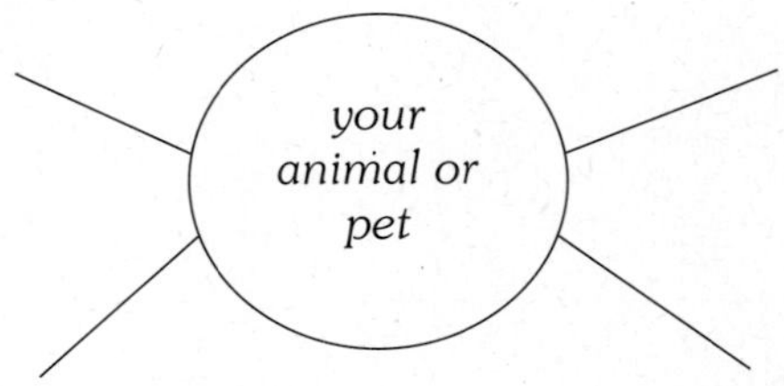

b) Write a similar stanza.

2. Fog

a) Read the poem *Fog* by Carl Sandburg and look up any words you don't know in a dictionary.

Fog
The fog comes
on little cat feet.

It sits looking
over harbor and city
on silent haunches
and then moves on

By Carl Sandburg, *Chicago Poems*, 1916.

b) Now think of another natural phenomenon (the weather, the stars, fields and forests, water, the earth, the seasons, etc.). Draw a circle in the middle of a piece of paper and write your choice of word in it.

c) Answer the following questions and arrange your answers around the word in the circle.
- Which animal could you use to describe your word?
- What size/colour/shape is it?
- What does it feel/smell/taste/look like?
- How would you describe its posture (the way it is sitting/standing)?
- When and how does it disappear?

d) Write a poem of your own which is similar to *Fog* using your answers to c).

Defining characters: A character poster

A character poster is a way of putting together information about a character. When you are reading a text, story or play, you can add information to your character poster as you read. When you have finished your poster, you can use the information to do a character study or to get an overall picture of what a character is like.

Step 1
Write the name of the character in the centre of your poster (or find a drawing, or a picture from a magazine).

Step 2
Arrange information about the character around the name/illustration in note form. Number the information if you want to show how a character changes or develops.

JOSH
(from: "Playing God", SB pp. 63–66)

1 fifteen or sixteen years old

2 he wants to run away from home

3 has a difficult relationship with his parents: they get angry with him about his grades, he thinks they don't care about him

4 thinks his parents blame him for the way their lives are

5 feels angry and neglected

6 is in love with Laurel

7 longs for care and understanding

8 feels worthless: thinks that nobody will miss him

9 wants to be cold and distant but is really loving and caring: he can't leave the puppies

10 learns to stand up for himself

11 begins to understand his father

Make a character poster for one of these characters from the student's book:
Mr Keating (pp. 72–73), the black-haired girl (pp. 82–83), the girl from 'Love stinks' (pp. 84–86) or Graham (p. 96).

How to write a personal letter

In a personal or informal letter, e.g. to a friend or relative, you can use informal language. Informal language is the kind of language you would use if you were speaking to the person. Here are some tips and phrases to help you structure your letter correctly.

Step 1
Write your own address, but not your name, in the top right-hand corner of the page. Write the date below the address.

Step 2
Start your letter: Dear *(Alex),*

Step 3
You can choose from the set phrases below to introduce new topics and link sentences. Remember to use connectives (see page 47) as well.

Step 4
Before you sign off (write your name) at the end of your letter use one of the informal phrases. (You can put one or more Xs after your name to send a kiss or kisses!)

3 The Thicket
Norwich

2nd March

Dear Cornelia,

Just a short note to let you know that I will definitely be coming to your school after the summer holidays. I had a letter from my host family, the Krügers, last week. They sound very nice. Do you know them?

Thanks very much for your last letter. I was pleased to hear you did so well in your last English test. Congratulations! I wish my German was as good as your English!

I'm sorry I haven't written for so long but unfortunately I was knocked off my bike on the way to college in January. I broke my right arm, which was very painful and I couldn't write for two months. Now it is almost better thank goodness.

I'm really looking forward to coming to Germany in September. Do you think you could write and tell me a bit about your school and especially about the courses that are available? As you know, our sixth form courses usually last for two years and we take between one and three subjects to A-level. I'm doing German, Business Studies and Economics. Is there a Business Studies course at your school?

Do write when you have time, and please give my love to the rest of your family. I'll be in touch again soon.

Lots of love,
Jill
XXXX

Useful phrases

For the beginning of your letter
- *Many thanks for …*
- *Thanks very much for …*
- *Sorry for not having written for so long.*
- *Just a short note to let you know …*
- *Just a few lines to let you know …*

Referring to the last news you received
- *I am/was glad to hear that …*
- *I am/I was very pleased to hear that …*
- *I am/was sorry to hear that …*

To introduce and link your news
- *I've been very busy recently because …*
- *Do you remember …?*
- *As you know, …*
- *Unfortunately …*
- *I'm sorry to say that …*
- *You won't believe what happened!*
- *All in all, …*
- *So really, …*
- *I'm looking forward to … (+ -ing)*

To finish your letter
- *Well, anyway, …*
- *That's (all) my news. What have you been up to?*
- *How are things with you?*
- *Drop me a line when you have time.*
- *I'll write again soon.*
- *Do write again soon!*
- *I'll be in touch again soon.*
- *Keep in touch.*
- *Give my regards to …*
- *Love from all the family.*
- *Give my love to …*

To sign off at the end of your letter
- *Best wishes,*
- *All the best,*
- *Love,*
- *Lots of love, …*

Read the letter in the example above. Imagine Jill is your penfriend. Write a letter back to her telling her about your school.

How to write a formal letter

In a formal letter (for example, if you apply for a job, need to order something or want to make a complaint) you should use formal language and structure your letter as described below. Read the steps carefully. The model letter is an application for a job as a voluntary worker for Oxfam (see advertisement, SB p. 95).

Step 1: First make notes about all the points you want to write about in your letter. Then arrange your points in order of relevance and priority (i. e. put the most important information first and the least important last).

Step 2: Write your address, without your name, in the top right-hand corner of the page. Write the date below your address.

Step 3: Write the name (if you know it) and address of the receiver on the left-hand side of the page starting on the line below the date. Don't forget the postcode! Write "Attn." (Attention) or "FAO" (for the attention of) in front of the name of the person you are writing to.

Step 4: State briefly what your letter is about, beginning with the abbreviation "Re: (referring to).

Step 5: Start your letter either:
Dear Mr/Mrs/Ms … ,
(if you know the person's name) or
Dear Sir or Madam,
(if you don't know the person's name)

Step 6: Write a short introduction in which you briefly say why you are writing. Begin the first paragraph with a capital letter. Here are some phrases which you could use:
- *I am writing to you about …*
- *I am writing for more information/further details about …*
- *With reference to your letter of* (+ date)/*your advertisement in* (+ name of newspaper, etc.) …
- *I would like to apply for …*
- *I would like to enquire about the possibility of* (+ -ing)

Step 7: Link your ideas with suitable connectives (see page 47) and phrases. The phrases below may be useful.
- *I would appreciate it if …*
- *I would be grateful if …*
- *I enclose a letter of recommendation …*
- *Please find enclosed* (*my CV/etc.*)

Step 8: At the end of the text, use a closing phrase. E.g.:
- *I look forward to hearing from you soon.*
- *Thank you very much in advance.*
- *I hope you will be able to help me.*

Step 9: Finish your letter either:
- *Yours faithfully,* (+ your name) or
- *Yours sincerely,* (+ your name)

Turmstr. 17
58566 Kierspe
Federal Republic of Germany

9th April 200…

Attn. Ms Baker
Oxfam
274 Banbury Rd
Oxford
OX2 7DZ

Re: Voluntary work in one of your shops or centres

Dear Ms Baker,

With reference to your advertisement in the *Third World Press* last month, I would like to apply for a job as a voluntary worker in one of your shops or centres in England.
I am 17 years old and I am in Year 11 at the Goethe Grammar School in Kierspe, Germany.
I have some experience of voluntary work as I have been helping in a "Dritte Welt Laden" in Germany for the last two years. My work there is very varied: I make window displays with clothes, artwork and posters, I work as a shop assistant and I sometimes serve food and drinks in the cafe.
I am good at organizing and I like working in a team: I have been team leader of a group of children in a church youth club since last summer.
I speak good English as I have been learning English at school for more than six years. However I would like to improve my English by spending some time in Britain.
Please find enclosed a copy of my CV[1] for your information and letters of reference from my school, the church youth club and the Dritte Welt Laden where I work.
I would be very grateful if you would consider me for a job in one of your centres.
I look forward to hearing from you soon. Thank you very much in advance.

Yours sincerely,

N. O. Name

[1] CV = Curriculum Vitae *(Lebenslauf)*

Write a formal letter on one of these topics:
a) to a holiday company complaining about a hotel.
b) to a software company asking for a holiday job.
c) to a summer camp offering to help. You could offer to give a surfing/tennis course or help with a playgroup, for example.

How to write a letter to the editor

A letter to the editor of a newspaper is a formal letter in which the reader comments on an article, event or opinion which has appeared in the newspaper. A letter to the editor is short and to the point and has the same formal beginning and ending as a formal letter (see page 41).

Step 1
Make notes about what you want to say and put these notes in a logical order.

Step 2
Briefly state which article/statements you are referring to. These phrases may help you:
- *With reference to your article of 1/6/200...* "(title/headline)"
- *In her article of 1/4/200...* "(title/headline)", *XX said ...*
- *I read XX's article of 1/4/200... with interest ...*

Step 3
Express your opinion clearly but politely, e.g. by
- using conditionals ('would'/ 'could'):
  I would appreciate (it if) ...
- asking questions instead of making statements:
  Why didn't the council inform us earlier?
- using the passive voice:
  We were not told of the change in the council's plans.

Step 4
Use intensifying adverbs (e.g *strongly, warmly, definitely*), connectives (see page 47) and subordinate clauses to structure your arguments. The connectives below will be particularly useful to you:
So • Thus • Therefore • To my mind • In my view • From my point of view • As a result • On account of • That is why • Consequently • All in all • Briefly • Taking everything into account

Step 5
Finish with a concluding paragraph in which you do one or more of the following:
- (re)state your opinion;
- summarize your findings;
- outline possible consequences;
- suggest that the reader makes up his/her own mind.

16 Knowle Avenue
Borehamwood
Herts
WD6 5FR

9th April 200...

The Editor
Borehamwood Post
Borehamwood
Herts
WD3 5HS

Re: Closing down of Langdon Road Youth Centre

Sir,

In your article of 1/4/200... "Langdon Road Youth Centre to close" it is said that the Youth Centre in Langdon Road is being closed because too few young people go there. Unfortunately your article forgets to explain why this is the case.
Firstly the centre is only open on Tuesdays and Thursdays from 5 pm to 8.30 pm. As many of us have other commitments (training, part-time jobs) at these times, we cannot go there then. In my opinion it would be better if the centre was at least open at weekends as well.
Secondly the facilities at the centre are in a very poor condition: the CD player has been broken for two months, the video recorder doesn't work and the pool tables are torn. Although we informed the council about the condition of the centre some time ago nothing has been done.
To my mind the council should talk with young people in the area and find out how the centre could be improved and made more attractive. Furthermore, if the Youth Centre is closed, even more young people in the area will be left out on the streets with nothing to do. As a result we can probably expect more vandalism and crime.

Yours sincerely,

Judith Homer

After reading the model letter above write a "letter to the editor" giving your opinion on the following matter:

You know that your local town council has been planning to build a roller skating centre on the outskirts of your town. Young people and families strongly support the plan. Local shop owners also welcome the idea as they can expect an increase in the number of visitors. However, some local residents are against the plan because they are worried about the increase in traffic and noise in their neighbourhood.
One morning you read an article in your local newspaper which says that the council has cancelled the project for the following reasons: The project can no longer be financed by public funds because of a sudden rise in other expenses; no company has been found which is willing to run the centre; a sponsor who promised to support the project has gone bankrupt; a well-known supermarket chain wants to buy the land and open a supermarket on it creating 50 new jobs.

How to make up a questionnaire

Often when you conduct a survey to find out people's views on a particular topic, it is helpful to use a questionnaire, i.e. a list of questions.

Step 1
Once you know the topic you want to investigate, brainstorm questions related to the subject. Don't ask too many questions – you don't want to put people off!

Step 2
Decide how the questions are to be put, i.e. whether they should be

- the open-ended type which ask for a free answer, e.g.
  What do you think of pollution?
- the agree/disagree type (with boxes to be ticked), e.g.
  Is there too much hysteria about the hole in the ozone layer?
  ❑ *yes* ❑ *no*
- the multiple choice type (with a choice of answers and boxes to be ticked), e.g.
  Recycling means
  ❑ *re-using things which have been thrown away.*
  ❑ *buying things which are second-hand.*
  ❑ *not buying things which are made of plastic.*
- the graded type (that can be answered on a three to five point scale), e.g.
  Shortages of natural resources will soon cause wars
  1 *definitely* **2** *possibly* **3** *definitely not*

Step 3
Arrange your questions in a clear and logical order. Don't forget to leave enough space for the answers!

Step 4
When you ask people to fill in your questionnaire, always remember to give them enough time to write down the answers!

Step 5
After people have filled in the questionnaires, decide how you are going to present the findings, e.g. as

- statistics, e.g.
  75% (of those asked) think there is not too much hysteria about the hole in the ozone layer
  40% …
- a graph or diagram

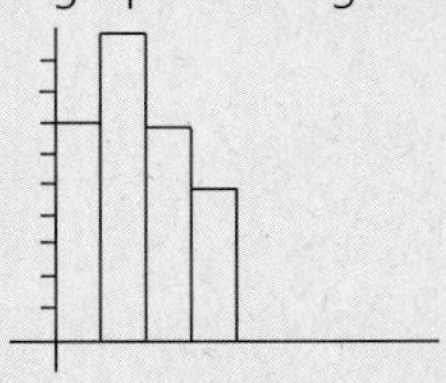

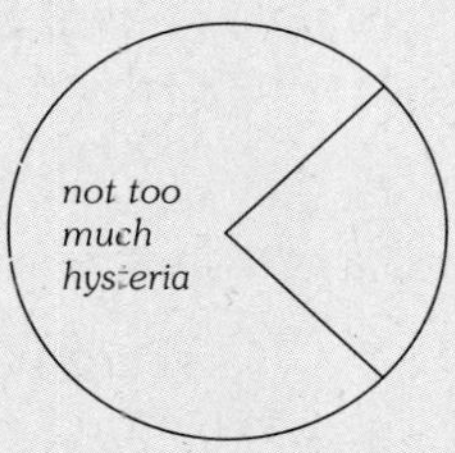

Work with a partner and make up a questionnaire about <u>one</u> of the following subjects. Your questionnaire should have 10 questions. Carry out your survey in class and then present your findings to your class.

<u>Either</u> a) What are you looking for in a job?
<u>or</u> b) How much do you care about the environment?
<u>or</u> c) What do you know about education/politics in Great Britain/the USA?

How to prepare and give a talk (see SB 107)

Preparation

Step 1: Brainstorm ideas on the topic you are going to talk about.

Step 2: Write keywords (but not complete sentences) on prompt cards which you can refer to while you are speaking. Arrange your prompt cards in a logical order E.g.
- from the least important to the most important idea
- in chronological order
- in antithetical order, i.e. giving an idea in favour followed by an idea 'against'.

Step 3: Think of an introduction that will catch your listeners' interest and attention and make a prompt card to go with it. You could start with:
- a provocative statement
- a question
- a short anecdote
- a joke
- a photo/picture/cartoon (on the OHP).

In your introduction you should also give a brief outline of what you are going to say so that the listeners know what to expect.

Step 4: In order to keep your listeners' attention throughout your talk make sure you:
- use interesting examples to explain and illustrate your main ideas
- use interesting language, structures and vocabulary to emphasize what you are saying (see page 47)
- use visual material, e.g. transparencies, writing on the board, maps, posters, flip charts, diagrams, etc.

You could add key words and phrases, etc. to your prompt cards to help you.

Step 5: Be concise. Try to form short, clearly structured sentences, and divide your talk into clear units.
(Don't forget, your listeners cannot re-read part of your talk if they don't understand it, so simplicity is very important.)

Step 6: Come to a convincing conclusion in which you summarize what you have said. Make a prompt card to go with your conclusion. This could be in the form of:
- a concluding paragraph
- a suitable quotation
- a short anecdote (if you didn't give one in the introduction).

Rules for giving a successful talk

1. *Plan your talk carefully (see Steps 1–6 on the left).*
2. *Talk to your listeners in a friendly and personal way.*
3. *Look at your listeners while you are talking!*
4. *Speak slowly and clearly.*
5. *Speak freely: Don't write your talk out in full and read it out. But do use prompt cards (see below and Steps 1–6).*
6. *Vary your tone of voice and expression so that you don't sound boring.*
7. *Appear confident, relaxed and self-assured.*
8. *Smile!*
9. *Encourage your listeners to ask questions at the end.*

Conclusion
- key words phrases
- quotation/anecdote
- vocab + phrases for reference

Point 3

Point 2
- key word/note

Point 1
- key word/note on point for reference
- example(s)
- vocab + phrases for reference

Introduction
- key words/phrases for telling (amusing) anecdote, etc.
- note on main points of talk
- vocab + phrases for reference

Prompt cards

Prepare a talk on 'friendship' based on one of the following proverbs and present your talk to your class.
- A friend in need is a friend indeed (= someone who helps you when you need it is a true friend)
- A hedge between keeps friendship green (= friends should always respect each other's privacy)
- Familiarity breeds contempt (= if you know too much about someone you don't respect them)
- Love is blind

How to hold a conversation (1) – Useful phrases

On this page you will find some tips which will help you to hold a conversation successfully in English. Read the words and phrases and make sure you understand all of them. Try to use them and follow the "rules" when you are having a conversation.

Opening a conversation

Hallo/Hi!
What are you doing?/What are you up to?
Do you mind if I join you?
Excuse me, …
Have you got time to …?
(I'm) sorry (to trouble you), but …
Could you (please) …?
Did you see … on TV yesterday/at the weekend/…?
Did you read about … in the paper?

"Rules" to remember

1. *Always be very polite when you talk to English-speaking people.*
2. *Speak clearly.*
3. *Try not to be abrupt or too direct.*
4. *Look at the person you are talking to.*
5. *Listen carefully to what the other person is saying and respond to it.*
6. *Try not to interrupt (too often).*

Expressing your opinion

In my opinion/view …
To my mind …
I think … (~~I mean~~)
I am sure/certain that …
I think/believe/feel that …
It seems to me that …
There should be …/ought to be …
I would like to …/I wouldn't like to …
It would be a good idea to … (because …)

Changing the subject

(Oh) by the way …
Before I forget …
I just thought of …
There's something else I wanted to ask you/say …
Oh, now I know what I wanted to say/ask you …
I know this has got nothing to do with what we are talking about, but …
Could I just say … (before I forget)?

Using fillers

Well. …
Actually …
You know/see …
Let's see …
I/you mean …
Now let me think/see.
In fact, …
I wonder …
The thing is …
I see what you mean.
Right then.
Let's say …

Interrupting

Wait a minute …
(I'm) sorry to interrupt, but …
Sorry, may I interrupt you for a second … ?
Sorry, but did you say …?
Can I just say/add that …
Yes/You're right/I agree, but …
I hope you don't mind, but …

Expressing surprise

I don't believe it!
That's strange/funny …
Are you being serious?
Are you pulling my leg?
Really?

Ending a conversation

OK, then …/Right …/So …
Well, anyway …
Would you excuse me now, please … ?
Sorry, but I've got to go now.
I'll see you soon/next week.
That's the way it goes./That's life.
You can't have everything, can you?
What would I do without you?
I hope everything goes well.
Look after yourself.
Take care.

Return to the original subject

As I was saying …
(Now) what was I saying/what were we talking about?
To get back to what we were talking about …
Let's get back to …
(Yes, well) anyway …

How to hold a conversation (2)

1. Practise the conversation below with a partner. One of you takes part A the other takes part B. Do not write down what you want to say. Use simple language and try to speak naturally. Use the phrases on pages 45 and 47 and remember to follow the rules!

Part A / **Part B**

A: It is breaktime at school. Your partner is reading a magazine. Greet him/her and start a conversation by asking what he/she is reading.

B: It is breaktime at school and you are reading a magazine. When your partner greets you, return the greeting and answer his/her question. You're reading an article about the homeless.

A: Ask B if he/she saw the programme on TV about the homeless last week.

B: You saw the programme. You found it interesting but your magazine article is more informative.

A: Give your opinion on the problem.

B: Change the subject: find out if A is still planning to go to England in the summer.

A: You aren't going away. You have got a job in a local firm.

B: You're surprised to hear this and want to know why A has changed his/her mind.

A: Explain why you aren't going to go to England, e.g. too expensive, you need money for a driving license, etc. Use fillers.

B: Express agreement or disagreement with A's explanation.

A: Try to end the conversation.

B: End the conversation.

2. Work in a group of 3 or 4 and have a conversation in which you talk about at least two of the following topics:

   a) what you did last weekend and what you are going to do together next weekend.
   b) an argument you have had with your parents recently because they say you don't help enough at home.
   c) your next/last English test.
   d) your opinion on a film/TV programme/music video which you have seen recently.
   e) your opinion on an important topic in the news at the moment (political/sports/local interest/disaster/etc.).

Connectives and adverbs

The following connectives and adverbs will help you to structure your writing and connect your thoughts and paragraphs logically.

Make sure you understand the words and phrases. Choose those you think you are most likely to use. Write them out in your own logical order.

To show order

to begin with • finally • firstly (secondly/ thirdly, etc.) • in the first/second/third place • initially • next

To express your own opinion

from my point of view • in my opinion• in my view • the way I see it • to my mind

To compare and contrast things

(al)though • both • but while the first … the second • compared to … • equally • likewise • on the one hand … on the other hand …

To express an opposite point of view

alternatively • but • despite/in spite of (the fact) • except for • however • in contrast to • instead of • nevertheless • nonetheless • on the contrary

To express reason and purpose

as • because of • consequently • for this/ that reason • hence • in order to • on account of • since • so • that explains why • that is why • therefore

To refer to something or someone

according to • as for • as to • the former • the latter • with reference to • with regard to

To express emphasis

as a matter of fact • at any rate • clearly • evidently • ideally • undoubtedly

To express or add ideas/to express agreement

admittedly • again • also • and • equally • for example • for instance • further(more) • in addition to • generally speaking • in the same manner/way • likewise • moreover • similarly

To express condition

as long as • even if • if • in any case • on condition that • provided that • unless

To show consequence and conclusion

accordingly • all in all • as a result • briefly • consequently • generally speaking • hence • in conclusion • it follows that • taking everything into account

Adverbs to tone down arguments

a little (worrying) • almost • fairly • hardly • more or less • quite • somewhat

Adverbs to emphasize arguments

actually • absolutely • (not …) at all • badly (needed) • completely • extremely • entirely • indeed • not in the least • perfectly • really • seriously • thoroughly • totally • utterly • very

Self-assessment: written production

This assessment sheet will help you to improve your writing skills and to avoid making careless mistakes. Tick the frequency that applies to you. Only consider the main ideas (in italics) – the examples only illustrate what is meant.

1. Before I start	**always**	**sometimes**	**never**
a) *I collect ideas,* e.g. I… brainstorm ideas – draw a diagram – make notes – make a mind map/topic web.			
b) *I find out what is typical of the text format* by looking in, e.g. my textbook – other sources (newspapers, magazines, etc.).			
c) *I make a plan to arrange my ideas in a clear and logical order,* e.g. for an essay – from the least important to the most important point or vice versa, or – in chronological order, or – in antithetical order, i.e. one argument followed by the opposite argument.			
d) *I make sure that every paragraph centres around a key idea,* e.g. there is – an introduction (short story: description of characters, setting, atmosphere; essay/formal letter/talk: a statement of the topic/question/quotation; newspaper article: a summary, an introduction); – a sequence of coherent paragraphs that contain the main text; – a concluding paragraph, (a formal letter: a closing phrase; an essay/a talk: a summary or conclusion; a short story: an ending).			

2. While I am writing	**always**	**sometimes**	**never**
a) *I match the style with the text format,* e.g. I use… – an expository or a factual style in a summary or an expository essay; – narrative and descriptive styles in a short story or newspaper article; – a mixture of persuasive and factual styles in an argumentative essay.			
b) *I use connectives* (see WB p. 47) *to give my ideas a clear and logical structure*, e.g. to show order – to compare/contrast things and ideas – to express ideas/opinions – to emphasize certain ideas.			
c) *I concentrate on the topic and avoid irrelevant ideas.*			
d) *I keep my language simple and use words I know.*			

3. After I finish writing and when I read through the text again	**always**	**sometimes**	**never**
a) *I check that I have covered all the ideas in my plan and used connectives to give my text a logical structure.*			
b) *I look at the vocabulary.* I check… my spelling – whether I have used words correctly.			
c) *I check the grammar.* I look at the… verb forms and tenses – position of adverbs and adjectives – use of the definite and indefinite article – syntax.			
d) *I check the style* (SB p. 121).			

Now count your points (always = 2 points, sometimes = 1, never = 0 points).

24–16: Your writing skills are admirable. You usually know how to structure a piece of writing and use the appropriate style. You know where to get help and how to check what you have written. Look at your results again and try to improve those skills that have scored you less than 2 points.

15–8: Your writing skills are improving. You already try to apply successful strategies. Look at your results again and concentrate on those skills that have scored you less than 2 points. Ask your teacher for help with the strategies which are new to you.

7–0: Lucky you – there is a whole new world ahead of you! Your writing skills will improve dramatically if you discover this new world. Look at the different strategies above and try to understand what is meant. Ask your teacher for help. Choose two strategies each from sections 1–3 and apply them in your next piece of writing. After that concentrate on a third strategy and then on a fourth one. Good luck!

How to present a music video in class

A music video is a short music film in which a song is interpreted visually. A music video is used to promote or market a song on TV or the internet.
Before you present your chosen video in class, you will need:
- *a taped version of the video and the lyrics*
- *useful vocabulary to help you talk about the lyrics and music (cf. SB p. 80)*
- *information about the band/singer. You could find biographical details and photos on the band's/singer's website, or record companies often provide information on the internet.*
- *activities to motivate your class to analyse the music video (cf. activity boxes at the bottom of this page).*

Step 1
Watch the video several times and note down your ideas about:
- content and message,
- the music,
- the pictures,
- the combination of sound and vision.

Step 2
Choose questions and activities from the activity boxes below which you can give to the class before, while and after viewing the video. Show the video to the class a few times.

Step 3
Prepare a worksheet for your viewers. They can then fill in their analysis results. Look at the table on the right for ideas.

<table>
<tr><th colspan="2">Name of song:</th><th>Singer/group:</th></tr>
<tr><td>content (lyrics)</td><td>ideas, images, recurring themes
plot
mood/atmosphere
message</td><td rowspan="3">combination of lyrics, music and pictures

Do the lyrics, music and pictures complement each other or are they different in some way?

What makes the pictures interesting? (E.g. unusual perspectives, an unexpected ending…)

What is the overall message of the video?</td></tr>
<tr><td>music</td><td>structure (stanzas, chorus/refrain)
instruments
rhythm</td></tr>
<tr><td>images</td><td>setting
characters
lighting techniques
camera operations
choreography
contrasts, e.g. colours, sequences, shots
special effects</td></tr>
</table>

Classify the music video (cf. SB p. 115)

Is it
… a *performance clip*? It concentrates on the music.
… a *concept performance clip*? It concentrates on music and visualized lyrics.
… a *concept clip*? It has a complex narrative or gives an associative interpretation of the song.
… a combination of different types?
… something completely different?

pre-viewing activities	while viewing activities	post-viewing activities
• Introduce the singer/group. • Watch the music video with the sound turned off. Try to guess what the lyrics are about. • Listen to the song without the picture. How would you visualize it in a video clip? • What ideas does the title of the song bring to mind?	• What functions do the camera operations have (cf. SB p. 112)? • Choose one still from the video. a) How does it reflect the atmosphere of the scene? b) Think up a caption for the still. • Write down words you can use to describe the characters in the video and their actions. • Does the video have a storyline? If so, summarize the story in a few sentences.	• How do the images used in the video relate to the lyrics? • What technical problems do you think the film crew might have had? • What recurring motifs/actions do you remember? What significance might they have? • What target group does the video clip appeal to? • If you had to design a music video poster, which still would you use? • How does the video appeal to you personally?

How to present a TV commercial in class

Step 1
Tape a commercial you consider worth watching. Note down what makes it effective (see box on the right for ideas).

Step 2
Decide which activities you would like to use to present the commercial in class. Look at the suggestions in the box at the bottom of the page.

Step 3
Divide the class into groups. Each group:
- summarizes how pictures, sound and text are used to convey the message,
- analyses which target group the commerical appeals to.

Then, compare results in class.

A TV commercial is an advertisement consisting of a short video narrative.

Analysing a commercial	
message	*e.g. product reflects values of today's youth…*
music, e.g. jingle, well-known song	
dialogue	
sound effects	
characters and roles	
pictures (colours, symbols, choreography)	
camera operations (see SB p. 112)	
editing, e.g. sequences of short/long shots	

Start your own dictionary of advertising!	
ad *short for* **advertisement**; public notice to market products/services **brand** kind of product made by a specific company **catch phrase** well-known phrase associated with a specific product	**jingle** a short, simple song or verse that can be easily remembered **logo** a printed symbol of a company **positioning** showing how a product is different from/better than another…

Factors	Target group
personal	*Describe the target group.* Age group: Interests/hobbies: Lifestyle:
cultural	*What cultural patterns are confirmed?* Values: Behavioural patterns: Likes/dislikes:
psychological	*Which ideas may influence the decision to buy? Note down ideas in direct speech.*
social	*Which social groups (family, peer group, clubs) or roles (leader, group member) affect the buying process?* Social groups: Roles:

pre-viewing activities	while viewing activities	post-viewing activities
• Collect ideas you associate with the product. • Suggest ideas (pictures and text) you would use to advertise the product. • Watch the commercial without the sound. What music, spoken text, etc. would you add? • Listen to the commercial without the picture. What images would you use?	• Stop the commercial after the first scene(s). What associations come to mind? • What roles, if any, do the characters play? • Concentrate on one still. a) What ideas do you think the still is supposed to convey? b) Think up a caption for the still.	• After watching the commercial once, note down everything you remember about it. • What image is given of the product? • What story, if any, is told in the commercial? • How does the commercial appeal to you personally? • Access http://www.adage.com to find out more about advertising trends.

How to present a news item in class

A news item is a single piece of news belonging to a news report. A news report consists of several news items presented by a newscaster.

If you want to find the latest news before it is published in the media, visit www.drudgereport.com with its links to well-known press agencies, TV channels and newspapers.

Start your own dictionary of media language!	
anchor s.o. who coordinates activities in a broadcast **bias** presentation of only one side of an argument or event **breaking news** latest news **to edit** to arrange images and spoken material into a suitable sequence **footage** film material **host** presenter of a TV or radio programme or show (except news programmes)	**overlap** the picture and sound complement each other **split** the picture and sound partly complement each other **sound-bite** a short, interesting sequence from a speech/interview, used to catch viewers' attention **wide split** picture and sound do not complement each other ......

Step 1
Tape news reports from American and British stations and compare them. Note the types of news you can distinguish. Is there a clear structure? (Cf. the table on the right for ideas.)

Step 2
Tape a topical news item. Prepare an analysis worksheet (cf. table below) and find out the effect of editing. Show the item to the class several times so they can analyse it in detail.

name of newscast:	**time:**
American / British channel:	
structure	What news items are covered? In what order?
studio sets	Which background screens, graphics, symbols, etc. are used? What is their effect?
newscasters	How many newscasters present the newscast? What is the function of the anchor?
presentation	How is information presented? (graphics, interviews, film, editorial comment, summary, studio discussion…)

topical aspects	visual material, pictures, e.g. film footage, graphics	spoken material, e.g. voice-over, dialogue, sound effects	editing: compare images and text (overlap/split/wide split)	camera operations (field size, camera angle, movement, position, cf. SB p. 112)	time in seconds
1.					
2.					

Step 3: Design your own evaluation sheet for news reports. You could use a ranking system like the one on the right.

• How impartial is the news report?	__ very __ partly __ biased
• How coherent are the individual news items?	__ very coherent __ partly __ incoherent
• How informative is the news item?	__ very __ partly __ uninformative
...	

Project: Covering a news item	
1. Choose a newsworthy story from a press agency and copy it for your group. (See www.drudgereport.com) 2. Collect ideas on how you could present the item for a TV news programme. Include visual material (statistics, maps, animated graphics, film footage, photos, etc.) and spoken material (interviews, studio discussion, voice-over for footage, sound-bites, etc.)	3. Arrange your ideas in a logical way. 4. Write texts for the newscaster(s): Include an introductory statement and introductions to reports, interviews, etc. 5. Write texts for the other formats (interviews, etc.) 6. Present your ideas in class and ask for feedback.

How to present a film in class

A feature film is a set of moving pictures produced for the cinema or TV. It is often based on a novel or other literary texts. In a film, images, sounds and language are arranged to produce a variety of meanings for the viewer.

Film genres
action – adventure – comedy – (crime) thriller – drama – fantasy – horror – mystery – romance – science fiction – Western

What makes a good film?
Collect 10 ideas in class and rank them from 5 (very important) to 1 (unimportant). Which ideas are the most important for the whole class? Consider, e.g.
characters – cast – plot (structure, key scenes, suspense) – setting (time and place) – atmosphere – symbols – special effects – camera operations – lighting – idea behind the film – impression the film made on you – soundtrack/music – dialogue – sound effects...

Step 1
Plan your film presentation and include some of the viewing activities in the boxes below.

Step 2
Decide how you want to show the film, e.g. in blocks of 30–45 minutes, in 4–10 segments.

Step 3
Note the results of the viewing activities in a file or on a poster or transparencies.

pre-viewing activities	while viewing activities	post-viewing activities
• Collect ideas as to what the film may be about. You can start a discussion with a film poster (from a video library) or show a key scene with the sound turned off. • Give a short outline of the plot of the film. Discuss how you would produce the film. You could consider the following points: themes – point of view – the beginning and ending of the film – the cast – the music.	• a) Choose a key scene. Make notes about the following: the relationships between the characters (cf. WB p. 53) – the techniques used to create audience empathy (cf. SB p. 113) – the setting – special effects (cf. SB p. 113) – the soundtrack, dialogues, etc. – camera operations (cf. SB p. 112) – the function of the scene in the development of the plot. b) Use your notes to illustrate the composition of the scene in a computer graphic or on a poster. • Choose one character and follow his/her experiences and relationships throughout the film. • Use a still and comment on one of the character's feelings.	• Find out more about the film on the internet. You could look for the ideas behind the film, how the film was received, interviews with the producer, director or actors, and for reviews, etc. • Write a film review (see WB p. 54) • What cultural knowledge do you gain from the film? • Compare the film version with the literary version. Consider: plot – characters – point of view.

Project: Designing a film poster for a class presentation

Steps
1. Watch a feature film in class.
2. Form groups and decide who does what (cf. box on the right).
3. Present your poster in class and compare your ideas.

Alternative:
1. Form groups and choose a film you want to present. Follow steps 1–3 above and design your poster.
2. Show the film in class and present your film poster.

Film title: **Starring:** **Plot summary** (see WB p. 36):	*Put a printout of a film review you wrote here (see WB p. 54).*
Put your analysis results here. plot – characters – camera operations and soundtrack	*Put your creative work here.* Choose a key scene and give your interpretation of it using any of the following formats: advertisement – collage – dialogue – debate – essay – interview – letter – news report – speech
Put your reaction to the film here. (E.g. how the film appeals to you, the experiences, aims and ideas you find important in the film)	

How to work with the characters in a film or novel

Films and novels tell stories in which characters go through major experiences. Film directors and novelists use different techniques to produce interesting characters: the film director uses carefully-edited pictures and sounds, the novelist uses carefully-narrated words. A viewer or reader must use his/her imagination and experiences to understand a character.

While viewing or reading I

Describe a character in a film or novel. You could use the character compass below in the following ways.

Film
- Choose a still and describe the character(s) in it.
- Pick a scene and describe how the character(s) are portrayed.
- Watch the whole film and make notes about one character. Then, present the character on a poster or collage.

Novel
- Look at the cover illustration. What information, if any, do you get about the character(s)?
- Pick a passage and describe the character(s) in it.
- Trace one character's development. Present a character profile on a poster or as a collage.

Film genres

Characters can assume one or more of the following roles in films and novels: good – evil – intermediary – hero – rival – villain – sidekick/assistant – butt of jokes – target of cruel humour – helper – henchman – uncritical follower – heroine – temptress – society

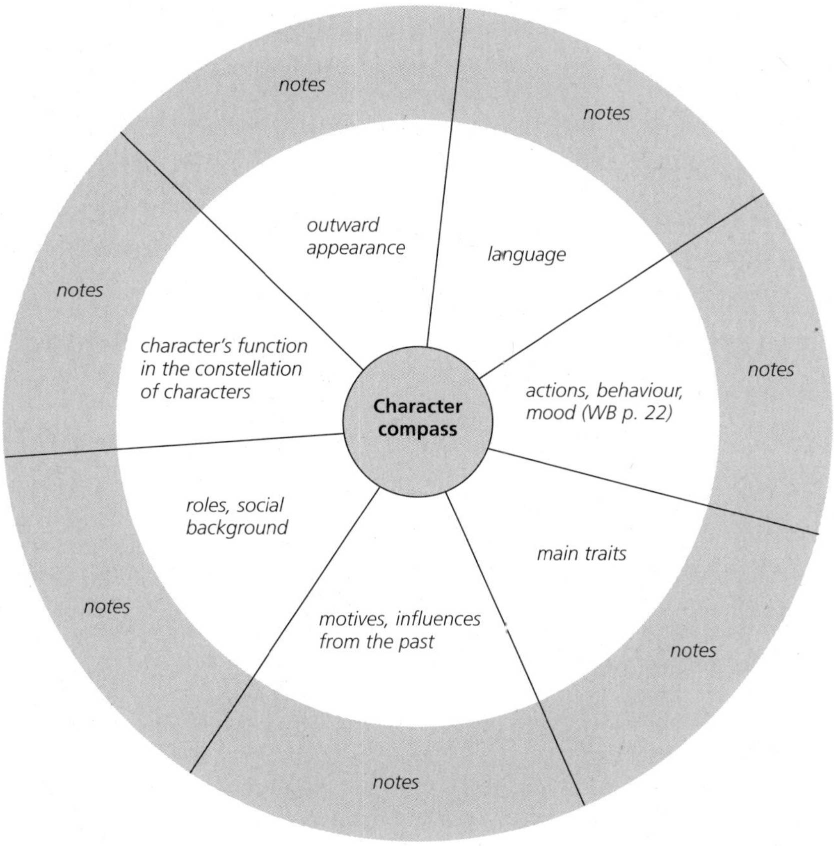

While viewing or reading II

Film: What effect does the cinematic point of view (see SB pp. 49, 113) have on how we see the characters? (E.g. "A subjective point of view makes me identify with X"…)

Novel: What effect does the narrative point of view have on how we see the characters? (Cf. SB pp. 27, 67.)

Further activities

Choose some questions and activities in the boxes below which you can give to your class before, while and after viewing the film.

pre-viewing activities	while viewing activities	post-viewing activities
• Show the class a film poster (from a video library) or book cover and ask for ideas about the film/novel. • Choose key sentences from dialogues and ask the class to predict the character constellation. • Give a one-sentence summary of the conflict and ask the class what characters they would choose to play different roles.	• Choose stills from one scene in the film and show how the point of view changes or remains consistent. • Find a caption for a key still. • Write an interior monologue for one character in a still or a scene. • Describe one character from another character's perspective. • Describe the function of camera operations in a scene (cf. SB, p. 112).	• Design a film poster or book cover, including the main characters. • Write a letter to a character from another character's point of view. • Which characters appeal to you most/least? • Check the internet for information about the film or novel.

How to write a film review

A film review is a report in which a film is assessed. Film reviews written for independent magazines and newspapers are usually critical, whereas the reviews written by cinema companies try to persuade readers to watch the film.

Step 1
Choose and watch a film you want to review. Make notes about:
- the names of the actors, director and producer,
- the film title and the author of the book if the film is based on a literary text,
- a summary of the plot in 3–5 sentences,
- what you feel to be the strengths and weaknesses of the storyline, cast, special effects, music, costumes, etc.

Step 2
Plan the structure of your review. Write it in a way that will arouse the reader's interest.
Title: Use a catchy phrase.
Opening paragraph: Plan this carefully. You could compare the film with similar ones, describe a problem the protagonist has to face, outline a spectacular scene, etc.
Main paragraph: Focus on plot, setting and characters.
Other paragraphs: Add interesting details, e.g. any awards, special effects, high production costs, etc.
Final paragraph: Come to a conclusion, e.g. give a final assessment, a recommendation, or not, an age rating.

Step 3
Revise your review. Use a factual and persuasive style, and connectives (see WB p. 47).

A–Z of useful words for film reviews

a amusing
b badly acted, boring
c complete waste of time, convincing
d dire
e entertaining, excellent
f far fetched theme, funny
g genuine characters, ghastly scenes
h heartbreaking, hilariously funny
i infuriating performance
l long-winded dialogues, lousy performance
m marvellous, melodramatic, moving
n noteworthy actors
o overacted
p promising production
q questionable plot
r realistic, remarkable, rubbish
s spectacular, stunning, superb
t thrilling
u unbelievable, unrealistic, unwatchable
v valuable, visionary insights
w weird characters
z zany

Project: Making a cinema magazine in class

A cinema magazine is produced to market topical films and persuade readers to watch them. It should include several film reports which provide detailed information. Each film report should include:
- a film review (cf. WB p. 53),
- a portrait of or a feature about the main actor/actress (see box below),
- photos (stills, posters from video libraries),
- an info box (see the box below right).

1. Before you start, decide on a layout (it must be the same for all groups). Consider, e.g. the cover of the magazine, the table of contents, the order of reports and the style and layout of a page. Choose someone to edit the whole magazine.
2. Work in groups. Choose a film you want to review.
3. Watch the film and divide the parts of the report (see 1. above) among group members.
4. Collect any extra material and write the texts. Then, discuss and revise your work in your group. Finally, provide a copy for the magazine editor.

How to portray a film star
1. Collect information from the internet and film magazines about the film star (his/her best films, career, personality, hobbies, family, etc.).
2. Write the portrait. Remember that you have to market the film star.
3. Add photos and captions to illustrate the portrait.

Info box	
Title: Country/year:	Length in minutes:
Director: Music by	Cameraman/-woman: Cast:
Soundtrack by Screenplay by	Internet links:

How to create an online film project

Step 1
Choose a short literary text and transform it into a video film. Consider the following points:
- What scenes/dialogues/characters can be omitted?
- What setting and background can be used?
- What camera operations can you use to express particular ideas?
- What cinematic point of view is best suited to your needs (see SB p. 113)?
- What symbols can you introduce to convey the message? (E.g. gestures, colours, objects, actions)

Step 2
Use the checklist below to organize your filmmaking project. Take the shots with a digital camcorder.

Step 3
Transfer the footage to the hard disk of your computer and use suitable software for the final cut and the sound.

Step 4
Compress the video film before you put it on your homepage. Write an introduction to the video.

Where can you get tools and software?
Ask your teacher for the address of the nearest *Filmbildstelle* to get advice and tools for your video production. *Filmbildstellen* also provide media workshops in which you can learn how to produce a video.

*****

What can you produce?
You can produce any of the following:
- a video of a literary text, e.g.
  - a short play/scene from a play (cf. SB "Keep on running" pp. 12–14; "Love stinks", pp. 84–86)
  - a short story (cf. SB "Mildred", pp. 21–26; "Playing God", pp. 63–68)
  - a poem (cf. SB "Growing up" p. 10)
  - a novel extract (cf. SB chapter two)
- a music video (see WB p. 49)
- a school documentary
- a traveller's guide to your hometown
- a video letter

Checklist for a filmmaking project

✔	Things to do	Who is in charge?
	– collect ideas, decide on genre and content – write a screenplay (include setting, characters, dialogue, some camera operations) – make a shooting script (a plan of how the film will be filmed; see box below) – draw a storyboard (the visualized shot-by-shot plan of a film) – find money to finance the film – direct the film (choose a cast; help actors to perform well; choose locations; decide on camera positions) – build sets, arrange the lighting – edit the film (put the filmed scenes into a specific order, order retakes)	

How to make a shooting script (see SB p. 112)

scene	picture content	field size	camera position	camera movement	camera angles	sound		
						dialogue	music	sound effects
1.								
2.								
3.								

Ideas for pre-, while and post-viewing activities

The boxes below provide ideas for presenting audio-visual media in class. The activities will keep you and the rest of the class actively involved in the presentation process. You can use the activities, e.g. to present key film scenes in a lesson, or as part of a 2–3-hour film workshop or in your film club.

Pre-viewing activities

Working with films
- Provide vocabulary lists and explanations to make it easier for viewers to understand a scene .
- Provide worksheets for viewers to fill in notes about characters, setting, plot, etc. (see WB p. 53)
- Use a film poster (e.g. from a video library) to get the class to speculate about the characters and plot.
- Choose key terms from film dialogues and ask the class to predict the character constellation and/or the story.
- Give a one-sentence summary of the conflict and ask the class what characters they would choose to develop the conflict.
- Give a short plot outline of the film. Collect ideas on how to produce the film.
  - What themes would you focus on?
  - What point of view would you choose?
  - What key scenes would you include? How would these scenes begin and end?
  - What actors, music, symbols, dialogues, camera operations and lighting would you use?

Working with commercials
- Name the product. Then, in class discuss what ideas you associate with it and how it could be marketed.
- Watch the TV commercial with the sound turned off. What sounds, music, spoken text, etc. would you add?
- Watch the commercial without the picture. What pictures would you use to accompany the text?

Working with music videos
- Watch the music video with the sound turned off. What might the lyrics be about?

While viewing activities

Working with films
- Choose a still and then,
  - describe the point of view (see SB p. 113),
  - think of a suitable caption,
  - comment on the character's/characters' feelings,
  - write an interior monologue for one of the characters,
  - describe the characters and the atmosphere,
  - explain the effect of the camera operations (see SB pp. 112–114).
- Choose a key scene. Illustrate its composition in a computer graphic or on a poster. Consider these points:
  - the relationships between characters (see WB p. 53),
  - the techniques used to achieve audience empathy (see SB p. 113),
  - the function of the setting: place, time, atmosphere,
  - the function of any special effects (see SB p. 113),
  - the effect of dialogues, music, sound effects, etc.
  - the function of camera operations (see SB p. 112),
  - the effect of this scene on plot development.
- Choose one character and accompany him/her through the film.
  - What experiences does he/she have?
  - How does he/she relate to the other characters?
- Comment on a scene with the sound turned off.
- Stop the film and ask for predictions. (What will happen next?)
- Show a scene from the film and ask for ideas about the plot up to then. (What happened before this point?)

Working with TV commercials
- Define the target group(s) the commercial appeals to.
- a) What is the message of the commercial?
  b) How do the pictures and the sound convey this message?

Post-viewing activities

Working with films
- How do you like the ending of the film? What other endings can you think of?
- Design a film poster. What aspects would you focus on?
- Suggest a different title for the film.
- Write a text for the back cover of the video version.
- Write a review of the film (see WB p. 54).
- Write a report for a cinema magazine (see WB p. 54).
- Make a storyboard for an additional scene (see SB p. 114).
- Compare the film with the literary version, if there is one. Which version do you think works better?
- Check the internet for:
  - background information about the film, e.g. www.imdb.com
  - interviews with the actors, director or producer.
- Write a *Facharbeit* in which you:
  - analyse a film, or
  - compare two films with a similar theme, or
  - compare a film with the novel it is based on.
- Make a collage about the film. Include material about the cast, characters and plot, photos, etc.
- Imagine you are interviewing one of the actors/actressess about his/her role in the film. Make up the interview.